City and Islington Sixth Form College
The Angel 283-309 Goswell Road
London EC1V 7LA
020 7520 0652

CITY AND ISLINGTON
COLLEGE

This book is due for return on or before the date last stamped below.
You may renew by telephone. Please quote the Barcode No.
May not be renewed if required by another reader.

Fine: 10p per day

7129

D1348019

Fourth Edition

 800 East 96th Street, Indianapolis, Indiana, 46240 USA

Sams Teach Yourself HTML in 10 Minutes

Fourth Edition

International Standard Book Number: 0-672-32878-x

Library of Congress Catalog Card Number: 2005909313

Printed in the United States of America

First Printing: May 2006

09   08   07   06   4   3   2   1

Trademarks

All terms mentioned in this book that are known to be trademarks or service marks have been appropriately capitalized. Sams Publishing cannot attest to the accuracy of this information. Use of a term in this book should not be regarded as affecting the validity of any trademark or service mark.

Warning and Disclaimer

Every effort has been made to make this book as complete and as accurate as possible, but no warranty or fitness is implied. The information provided is on an "as is" basis. The author and the publisher shall have neither liability nor responsibility to any person or entity with respect to any loss or damages arising from the information contained in this book.

Bulk Sales

Sams Publishing offers excellent discounts on this book when ordered in quantity for bulk purchases or special sales. For more information, please contact

U.S. Corporate and Government Sales
1-800-382-3419
corpsales@pearsontechgroup.com

For sales outside of the U.S., please contact

International Sales
international@pearsoned.com

ACQUISITIONS EDITOR	Betsy Brown
DEVELOPMENT EDITOR	Songlin Qiu
MANAGING EDITOR	Charlotte Clapp
PROJECT EDITOR	Andy Beaster
COPY EDITOR	Ben Berg
INDEXER	Heather McNeill
PROOFREADER	Mike Henry
TECHNICAL EDITOR	Gary Rebholz
PUBLISHING COORDINATOR	Vanessa Evans
INTERIOR DESIGNER	Gary Adair
COVER DESIGNER	Aren Howell
PAGE LAYOUT	TnT Design, Inc.

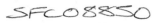

10.99

Contents

About the Author

Deidre Hayes is an information architect with a Web services group that created and manages a very successful corporate intranet. She is continually looking for ways to increase productivity with online workflow technologies and has spoken to national audiences on her favorite Web-related topics: information design and usability. She is a member of the Society for Technical Communications, the Usability Professionals Association, and the HTML Writers' Guild.

Acknowledgments

I would like to thank my family—especially my beautiful daughter, Alexandra—for their patience. Thanks to my friends and colleagues for challenging me everyday. And, thanks also to the editing staff at Sams Publishing for their dedicated help.

We Want to Hear from You!

As the reader of this book, *you* are our most important critic and commentator. We value your opinion and want to know what we're doing right, what we could do better, what areas you'd like to see us publish in, and any other words of wisdom you're willing to pass our way.

You can email or write me directly to let me know what you did or didn't like about this book—as well as what we can do to make our books stronger.

Please note that I cannot help you with technical problems related to the topic of this book, and that due to the high volume of mail I receive, I might not be able to reply to every message.

When you write, please be sure to include this book's title and author as well as your name and phone or email address. I will carefully review your comments and share them with the author and editors who worked on the book.

Email: webdev@samspublishing.com

Mail: Mark Taber
           Associate Publisher
           Sams Publishing
           800 East 96th Street
           Indianapolis, IN 46240 USA

Reader Services

Visit our website and register this book at www.samspublishing.com/register for convenient access to any updates, downloads, or errata that might be available for this book.

Introduction

If you're reading this book, you must have some idea of what HTML is, right? Maybe you already know that HTML is the language of the Internet and that far from being a complex programming language requiring years to perfect, HTML is actually a simple markup language that you can learn very quickly. XHTML is the latest version of HTML. You'll learn more about how these two standards work together to create Web pages in later chapters.

You're probably thinking that if you knew how to create documents in HTML, you could help your company earn more money, or better yet, help you earn more money.

What you probably don't know is how to get started. How do you learn that language and what's it going to cost?

What You Need to Know Before Using This Book

Guess what? You can create HTML documents on any computer system because HTML works the same on any type of computer. Even better, you can use software that you already own to do it. Any kind of text editor (such as Microsoft Notepad) can be used.

Because we're covering a lot in 10 minutes, it will certainly help as you go through this book if you already have some basic computer skills (including the ability to use a word processor, some understanding of how to use directories and filenames on your computer system, and some experience using a Web browser such as Netscape or Internet Explorer).

About the *Sams Teach Yourself in 10 Minutes* Series

Sams Teach Yourself HTML in 10 Minutes uses a series of lessons that walk you through the basics of HTML, and then moves on to more advanced features of the language. Each lesson is designed to take about

10 minutes and each is limited to a particular feature, or several related features, of the HTML language. There are plenty of examples and screen shots to show you what things look like. By the time you finish this book, you should feel confident in creating your own HTML documents for the World Wide Web. You can even use HTML to provide unique and valuable services to your organization, or to tell the world about yourself.

Special Sidebars

In addition to the explanatory text and other helpful tidbits in this book, you will find icons that highlight special kinds of information.

Plain English sidebars appear whenever a new term is defined. If you aren't familiar with some of the terms and concepts, watch for these flagged paragraphs.

Caution sidebars alert you to common mistakes and tell you how to avoid them. These paragraphs also explain how to undo certain features, and highlight differences between HTML and XHTML.

Tip sidebars explain shortcuts (for example, key combinations) for performing certain tasks.

Note sidebars present pertinent pieces of information related to the surrounding discussion.

Conventions Used in This Book

The creation and editing of HTML documents can be done using any one of a wide variety of editing tools. You'll find many excerpts from HTML documents that illustrate the points being made. These fragments look like this:

```
<html>
<head><title>This is the Title of Your Page</title></head>
<body>This is the document text surrounded
by HTML tags.</body>
</html>
```

If you're working along with the examples, you might want to enter the HTML fragments into your own HTML documents as you move through the lessons.

Web Browser Screen Shots

Web browsers (such as Internet Explorer and Netscape) are used to interpret HTML documents for your computer. There are many different types of Web browsers (some with more bells and whistles, some with less), but they all do essentially the same thing. You'll find out about some of these differences (and how to avoid problems) as we move through the lessons in this book. To avoid confusion, all the Web browser screen shots in this book were taken from Internet Explorer.

LESSON 1
What's It All About?

In this lesson, you will learn how the Internet works and why HTML and XHTML are so important.

What Is the Internet?

Like many inventions, the Internet began as the solution to a problem. It began with the government's need to find a way to link several computer networks together so that files could be shared. In other words, it created a network of networks. These computer networks were located all over the world and sharing information the old-fashioned way took a long time. Today, the idea of sharing files with people around the world doesn't sound like such a big deal when almost everyone has the modem, e-mail, and dial-up connections that make *Wide Area Networks* (*WANs*) commonplace. Back then, however, no one had even considered the idea. So, how did they do it? Well, researchers working for the *Advanced Research Projects Agency* (*ARPA*) created ARPAnet, which became the first WAN. Eventually, this led to an *Internet Protocol (IP)*—a common computer language—enabling all computers to talk to each other.

 Internet Protocol (IP) A predefined set of rules used to enable computers to communicate with each other, regardless of which operating system they are running.

This protocol and the new network of networks made exchanging information much easier than ever before, but it still wasn't simple. To find information on the Internet, you had to know where it was stored. You first had to understand how all the computers were connected, and then you had to navigate through the network to find the data you were looking for.

All that changed in the early 1990s. At that time, a new protocol was created. That protocol, the *Hypertext Transfer Protocol (HTTP)*, enabled information on the Internet to be accessed from *anywhere*, by *anyone*. It's what allows you to jump from one Web page to another by pointing and clicking. The code that makes up the HTTP was a breakthrough, but it can't do everything by itself. The information stored on the computers in the network (the documents and data) must include its own set of communication tools so that the other computers in the network can interpret it. In the case of the World Wide Web, the communication tool is *HTML*.

 HTML   Stands for *Hypertext Markup Language*. Most documents that appear on the World Wide Web were written in HTML.

What Is HTML?

In the Introduction, you learned that HTML is a markup language, not a programming language. In fact, the term *HTML* is an acronym that stands for *Hypertext Markup Language*. You can apply this markup language to your pages to display text, images, sound and movie files, and almost any other type of electronic information. You use the language to format documents and link them together, regardless of the type of computer with which the file was originally created.

Why is that important? You know that if you write a document in your favorite word processor and send it to a friend who doesn't have that same word processor, your friend can't read the document, right? The same is true for almost any type of file (including spreadsheets, databases, and bookkeeping software). Rather than using some proprietary programming code that can be interpreted by only a specific software program, HTML is written as plain text that any Web browser or word processing software can read. The software does this by identifying specific elements of a document (such as heading, body, and footer), and then defining the way those elements should behave. These elements, called *tags*, are created by the *World Wide Web Consortium (W3C)*. You'll learn more about tags in upcoming lessons.

Tags   These are elements of a Web page that are used to define how those pages should behave. They are most often used in pairs, which surround the element they are defining.

World Wide Web Consortium (W3C)   Members of this group develop the protocols that make up the World Wide Web. Currently, the W3C has 180 members from commercial, academic, and governmental organizations worldwide.

Then, What's XHTML?

XHTML, an acronym for *eXtensible Hypertext Markup Language*, is the first big change to HTML in years. With it, the W3C is trying to add the structure and extensibility of *XML* to HTML pages. By adding a few simple structural elements to existing HTML pages, you can be assured that your Web pages are compatible with later versions of HTML, and even with XML. Lesson 2, "Creating Your First Page," has all the information you need to get started.

XHTML   Stands for *eXtensible Hypertext Markup Language*. It is the next generation of HTML.

XML   Stands for *eXtensible Markup Language*. It is the newest language being developed by the W3C, and is also the most flexible. You'll learn more about it in Lesson 17, "Planning for the Future."

How Do They Work?

Markup languages such as HTML and XHTML serve another important purpose when it comes to sharing information over long distances: Information comes to you faster because your computer (using a Web browser) does the work of interpreting the format of the information after you receive the page. Sound confusing? Well, let's look at it another way.

Your computer has a Web browser, such as Internet Explorer or Netscape Navigator, installed on it. When you are looking for information on the Web, your browser has to find the computer that is storing that information. It does this using the HTTP. The storage computer, or server, then sends the new Web page (as a plain text file) back to your computer using the same HTTP. Your browser sees the new Web page and interprets the text and HTML tags to show you the formatting, graphics, and text that appear on the page.

 Tip   HTTP isn't the only protocol used on the Internet. Each protocol is used for a specific network service, such as electronic mail or file transfers.

Using Web Browsers

As great as Web browsers are, you should be aware of some limitations. Although all HTML commands are the same, not all browsers interpret the commands in the same way. Some browsers, such as Lynx, can display only text (even if the HTML author added images to the document). Some older browsers do not understand the newer HTML commands and might produce errors rather than text. What's more, some of the newest browsers enable viewers to determine which window display sizes, fonts, and colors they prefer when viewing Web pages (even if those settings are different from what you, the Web author, want them to see). Don't despair; there is good news. Most Web pages look the same, or almost the same, on every browser regardless of the computer system: PC, Macintosh, or UNIX. With each lesson in this book, you'll find tips to help ensure that your pages are viewed as you intended. Keep these tips in mind as you create your own Web pages, and you'll avoid the disappointment that many novice Web authors face as they realize that the page they worked so hard on looks awful on another computer or browser.

Tip   The Web itself offers Web page designers the opportunity to preview their pages on a number of different browsers at one time. Web sites, such as AnyBrowser (www.anybrowser.com), show you exactly how each browser will interpret your page. You can use this information to redesign your page and help ensure that most people see it the way you intend.

Getting Connected

This might be apparent, but sometimes it pays to state the obvious: Although you can create Web page files in any plain text editor and view them in any browser, you have to decide how you are going to store the files. You already know that you can't surf the Net without having an *Internet Service Provider (ISP)*. In the same way, you need a *Web Presence Provider (WPP)*—or your own Web server—to store your pages before they can be viewed from the Web. Other ways to view Web pages also exist. Table 1.1 describes the methods you can use to store your files.

TABLE 1.1   Storing and Viewing Your Documents

If You Store Your Files On	They Can Be Viewed by People with Access To
Your own computer	Your computer (or an intranet)
A disk or CD-ROM	That disk or CD-ROM
A Web host server	The World Wide Web

Internet Service Provider (ISP) A company that provides you with access to the Internet.

Intranet This is like your own private Internet in that it uses the same HTTP as the World Wide Web, but it is accessible only by people within your own network.

Web Host A company that stores (hosts) information that can be accessed from the Internet using the HTTP. A Web host may also be called a *Web Presence Provider (WPP)*.

In this lesson, you've learned:

- HTML and XHTML are markup languages that define the structure, rather than the format, of the text elements in your documents.

- HTML is platform independent. As long as they have a browser, your Web site visitors can see the same Web page on a PC, a Macintosh, or a UNIX computer.

- XHTML, the latest version of HTML, requires more structure than HTML.

- You need a Web server or a Web Presence Provider to store your pages before they can be viewed from the Web.

LESSON 2
Creating Your First Page

In this lesson, you will learn to create, save, and view simple Web pages.

Getting Started

I think you'll find that the best way to learn is to follow along with the examples in this book and create your own Web pages as you read. As you learned in the introduction of this book, you can create Web pages or HTML documents with any text editor (including Microsoft Notepad, DOS edit, Mac SimpleText, and UNIX vi). You probably already have at least one of these editors installed on your computer, even if you have never used it before.

Caution Although you can also create Web pages using some word processors (such as Microsoft Word) and some *WYSIWYG* programs (such as Microsoft FrontPage), I suggest that you ignore these programs for now and concentrate on learning HTML. HTML authoring tools are discussed in Lesson 15, "Using Web Authoring Tools."

WYSIWYG An acronym for *What You See Is What You Get*. It generally refers to software programs that enable you to see what the page looks like without seeing all the program's formatting codes.

Required Elements

To see what HTML looks like and learn the most basic HTML tags, let's look at a very simple HTML document. Figure 2.1 shows a simple Web page in Microsoft Notepad. You can type the same text in your own editor to follow along with the lesson.

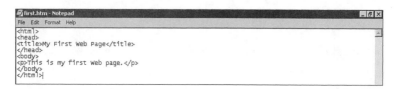

FIGURE 2.1   The <html> and </html> tags are all you need to identify your file as an HTML file.

Every HTML document must begin with the <html> tag and end with its complement, the </html> tag. In addition to the <html> tag, this document includes three other pairs of tags that should be included in any HTML document:

- The <head> and </head> tag pair is used to indicate any information about the document itself. You'll learn how to add some of this information in later lessons.

- The <title> and </title> tags are used to add a title to your browser's Title bar. The Title bar is the colored band at the top of any application that gives the name of the application.

- The <body> and </body> tags are used to surround any text that appears in the HTML page.

All HTML documents are separated into two parts: the head and the body. Because the title contains information about the document, the <title> and </title> tags are placed within the <head> and </head> tags.

One More Page

If you were to create another simple HTML page, you would see that the same four tags are present in this document as well. Only the text that appears between tags is changed.

```
<html>
<head>
<title>My Second Web Page</title>
</head>
<body>
<p>This is my second Web page.</p>
</body>
</html>
```

 Tip   Most HTML tags come in pairs. You use the first tag in the pair (for example, <html>) to tell the computer to start applying the format. The second tag (for example, </html>) requires a slash in front of the tag name that tells the computer to stop applying the format. The first tag is usually referred to by the name within the bracket (for example, *HTML*). You can refer to the second tag as the end, or the close, tag (for example, *end HTML*).

Saving and Viewing the Page

To view your own page in a browser, you must first save it. Because you've created an HTML document, you want to save your file with an .htm extension (first.htm, for example) so that you recognize it quickly.

 Caution   Some people prefer to name their HTML files with an .html extension (for example, first.html). Some older computer systems, however, still require the file extension to be three characters or fewer and might have trouble reading (or storing) a file with a longer extension.

You can preview any HTML file in your browser, even when that file is stored on your computer rather than on a Web server. In Internet Explorer, you can view your new file by selecting Open from the File menu. Figure 2.2 shows how Internet Explorer displays the first.htm file that you created in Figure 2.1.

Tip   Although you don't see them, HTML commands are sitting behind the scenes of every document that you open in your Web browser. You can see the HTML commands by selecting Source from the View menu of Internet Explorer (other browsers might use different menu commands). When you find a page on the Web that you like, you can view the source code to learn how you can use HTML to create something similar.

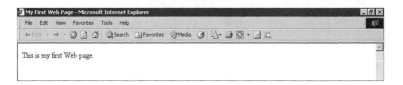

FIGURE 2.2   My First Web Page as it appears in the Internet Explorer browser. Notice that the Title bar contains the text between the <title> and </title> tags and the body of the browser contains the text between the <body> and </body> tags.

Caution   Some Web pages use frames to display more than one HTML page at the same time. (See Lesson 10, "Creating Frames.") To view the source code for this type of page, make sure that you use your mouse to highlight some portion of the page you're interested in before selecting Source from the View menu.

XHTML Requirements

XHTML, the latest revision of HTML, adds another required element to your Web pages: the <!DOCTYPE> tag. This tag appears at the top of the file and identifies the file as an HTML document conforming to the XHTML requirements. If you were to create an XHTML-conforming document, it would look like the following:

```
<!DOCTYPE html
      PUBLIC "-//W3C//DTD XHTML 1.0 Transitional//EN"
      "http://www.w3.org/TR/xhtml1/DTD/xhtml1-
transitional.dtd">
<html xmlns="http://www.w3.org/1999/xhtml"
      xml:lang="en" lang="en">
<head>
<title>My XHTML Page</title>
</head>
<body>
<p>This is my first XHTML page.</p>
</body>
</html>
```

The `<!DOCTYPE>` tag has three variations: Strict, Transitional, and Frameset. You declare which one you are using in the top of the file.

- **Strict**   Declare this variation when you are certain that your viewers will be accessing your pages from newer browsers that interpret style sheets correctly. You'll learn more about style sheets in Lesson 5, "Adding Your Own Style." The Strict variation looks like this:

```
<!DOCTYPE html
      PUBLIC "-//W3C//DTD XHTML 1.0 Strict//EN"
      "http://www.w3.org/TR/xhtml1/DTD/xhtml1-strict.dtd">
```

- **Transitional**   Declare this variation when you are not certain how your viewers will be accessing your pages.

```
<!DOCTYPE html
      PUBLIC "-//W3C//DTD XHTML 1.0 Transitional//EN"
      "http://www.w3.org/TR/xhtml1/DTD/xhtml1-
      transitional.dtd">
```

- **Frameset**   Declare this variation when you are working in frames. You will learn more about frames in Lesson 10.

```
<!DOCTYPE html
      PUBLIC "-//W3C//DTD XHTML 1.0 Frameset//EN"
      "http://www.w3.org/TR/xhtml1/DTD/xhtml1-
      frameset.dtd">
```

Caution This book uses the Transitional variation of the <!DOCTYPE> tag throughout. It's a good habit to get into, allowing you to conform to W3C rules, but offering more flexibility that the Strict variation.

You might have noticed one more change from the HTML required elements: The <html> tag has some new attributes: xmlns, xml:lang, and lang. In HTML, you only have to include the <html> tag to identify the document as an HTML file, but XHTML requires that you use the xmlns attribute to link your document to the W3C's definition of XHTML, which continues to evolve. You will learn more about this evolution and how to prepare for it in Lesson 17, "Planning for the Future." For now, just remember to include the <!DOCTYPE> tag and the full <html> tag (shown in the following sample) in all your Web pages. Figure 2.3 demonstrates how the XHTML page, created previously, would appear in the browser.

```
<!DOCTYPE html
     PUBLIC "-//W3C//DTD XHTML 1.0 Transitional//EN"
     "http://www.w3.org/TR/xhtml1/DTD/xhtml1-
     transitional.dtd">
<html xmlns="http://www.w3.org/1999/xhtml"
     xml:lang="en" lang="en">
```

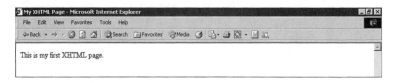

FIGURE 2.3 Notice that adding the XHTML declaration does not affect your page's appearance.

Caution The <!DOCTYPE> tag is the only tag that appears in uppercase. All other HTML tags should be lowercase as explained in the next section.

Using Good Form

Tags aren't the only things that make a good Web page. As you continue through the lessons in this book, you'll discover that while HTML was very forgiving, XHTML must conform to the rules. Though current versions of the most popular browsers will recognize your intentions even if you use incorrect tags (or enter the correct tags in the wrong order), later versions will not. You'll want to move beyond the novice level now and follow some basic Web coding principles to conform to XHTML's standards. Following is a brief list of those principles, but you'll learn more in later lessons:

- *Include all the required XHTML elements that you learned in this lesson*   You might want to create a template for yourself that already includes these tags. You can use the XHTML document created in the "XHTML Requirements" section as a template. Whenever you create a new Web page; open your template file, add your new text, and save the new file.

- *Use lowercase for all tags*   To the browser, <HEAD>, <Head>, and <head> all mean the same thing. (That won't always be true.) Use the same lowercase spelling for all your commands and you won't be caught having to recode your pages as the standard evolves.

- *Never use spaces in filenames*   Older computer systems have trouble reading filenames that include spaces (for example, *my first page.htm*). Instead, you can use a couple of file management tricks to replace the spaces:

    - Use an underscore (_) to represent spaces (for example, my_first_page.htm).

    - Use initial capital letters to indicate new words in a filename (for example, MyFirstPage.htm).

Table 2.1 shows a list of the tags that you learned in this lesson. A similar table of new HTML tags appears at the end of other lessons.

TABLE 2.1   HTML Tags Used in This Lesson

HTML Tag	Closing	Description of Use
`<!DOCTYPE>`		Begins each XHTML document and includes a reference to the Strict, Transitional, or Frameset variation.
`<html>`	`</html>`	Surrounds all the text in an HTML file. XHTML documents must include the `xmlns`, `xml:lang`, and `lang` attributes.
`<head>`	`</head>`	Contains information about the document. Must include the `<title>` tag.
`<title>`	`</title>`	Identifies the title of the page.
`<body>`	`</body>`	Surrounds the text of the page.

In this lesson, you've learned:

- Any text editor, including Microsoft Notepad, can be used to create Web pages (or HTML documents).

- All HTML documents are separated into two parts: the head and the body.

- Every HTML document must include the `<html>` tag and end with its complement, the `</html>` tag.

- Every XHTML document must include a valid variation of the `<!DOCTYPE>` tag before the `<html>` tag.

- All HTML tags (except the `<!DOCTYPE>` tag) should be typed in lowercase.

LESSON 3

Adding Text and More

In this lesson, you will learn how to use HTML to add text and headings in your Web pages. You'll also learn how to add mathematical notations, information about your Web page, and special characters (such as ampersands).

Paragraphs

You might not realize it, but you already learned how to create an HTML paragraph in Lesson 2, "Creating Your First Page." In HTML, a paragraph is created whenever you insert text between the <p> tags. Look at the code from Lesson 2 again:

```
<!DOCTYPE html
    PUBLIC "-//W3C//DTD XHTML 1.0 Transitional//EN"
    "http://www.w3.org/TR/xhtml1/DTD/xhtml1-
    transitional.dtd">
<html xmlns="http://www.w3.org/1999/xhtml"
    xml:lang="en" lang="en">
<head>
<title>My XHTML Page</title>
</head>
<body>
<p>This is my first XHTML page.</p>
</body>
</html>
```

Web browsers see that you want text and they display it. Web browsers don't pay any attention to how many blank lines you put in your text; they only pay attention to the HTML tags. In the following HTML code, you see several lines of text and even a blank line, but the browser only recognizes paragraphs surrounded by the <p> and </p> tags (or paragraph tags). The <p> tag tells the browser to add a blank line before displaying any text that follows it, as shown in Figure 3.1.

```
<!DOCTYPE html
        PUBLIC "-//W3C//DTD XHTML 1.0 Transitional//EN"
        "http://www.w3.org/TR/xhtml1/DTD/xhtml1-
        transitional.dtd">
<html xmlns="http://www.w3.org/1999/xhtml"
        xml:lang="en" lang="en">

<head>
<title>Typing Paragraphs in HTML</title>
</head>
<body>
<p>This is the first line.

But is this the second?</p>
<p>No, this is.</p>
</body>
</html>
```

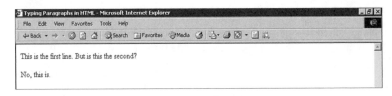

FIGURE 3.1   The browser ignores the blank line that I inserted and puts the line break before the <p> tag instead.

Web browsers do something else with paragraph text that you should be aware of: They wrap the text at the end of the browser window. In other words, when the text in your Web page reaches the edge of the browser window, it automatically continues on the next line regardless of where the <p> is located.The <p> tag always adds a blank line, but you might not always want a blank line between lines of text. Sometimes you just want your text to appear on the next line (such as the lines of an address or a poem). You can use a new tag for this—the line break, or <br /> tag, shown in Figure 3.2.

This new tag forces the browser to move any text following the tag to the next line of the browser, without adding a blank line in between. Figure 3.3 shows how the browser uses these two tags to format your text.

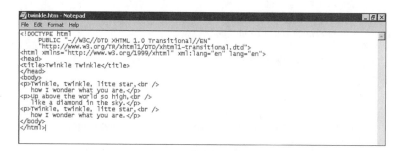

FIGURE 3.2   The `<p>` and `<br />` tags help to separate your text into lines and paragraphs.

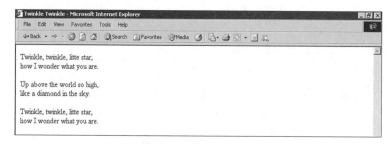

FIGURE 3.3   The browser inserts line breaks and blank paragraph separators only where you place the correct HTML tags.

Text Emphasis

So far you've learned how to add text, but here you will learn how to format it. You will occasionally want to add emphasis to your text to make it stand out. HTML enables you to quickly apply some standard formats, such as boldface and italic, using a predefined set of tags. All these tags occur in pairs (corresponding opening and closing tags) and must surround the text that they are emphasizing. Use the code that follows in your own Web page to see how each of these tags appears in the browser.

```
<!DOCTYPE html
        PUBLIC "-//W3C//DTD XHTML 1.0 Transitional//EN"
        "http://www.w3.org/TR/xhtml1/DTD/xhtml1-
        transitional.dtd">
```

```html
<html xmlns="http://www.w3.org/1999/xhtml"
      xml:lang="en" lang="en">
<head>
<title>Emphasizing Text</title>
</head>
<body>
<p>Make your text one size larger with the
   <big>big tag.</big></p>
<p>Try the <b>bold tag</b> or the <strong>strong tag</strong>
   to make an impact.</p>
<p>The <i>italics tag</i> and the <em>emphasis tag</em>
 create a different impact.</p>
<p>Use the <tt>teletype tag</tt> to imitate a typewriter.</p>
<p>Make your text one size smaller with the
   <small>small tag.</small></p>
</body>
</html>
```

 Caution   Other formatting tags exist in HTML, but their use is discouraged in HTML and deprecated in XHTML in favor of style sheets. The World Wide Web Consortium (W3C) has determined that HTML should be used to identify types of information (text, headings, tables, and so on), but should not be used to format that information.

 Deprecated   Some older HTML tags, specifically related to formatting, have been replaced by the formatting capabilities of style sheets.

Style Sheets   Web developers use style sheets to specify formatting instructions for a single document or a group of documents.

You'll learn how to create style sheets in Lesson 5, "Adding Your Own Style." Throughout the book, however, you'll see how styles can enhance your Web pages.

Headings

Separating your text into paragraphs isn't the only way to format your Web pages. HTML enables you to add six different heading tags to your pages by using the tags <h1>–<h6>. These tags are very simple to use. Look at the following line of code:

```
<h1>This is Heading 1</h1>
```

The closing heading tags also create an automatic paragraph break. In other words, all headings automatically include a blank line to separate them from the text. Heading 1, the <h1> tag, has the largest font of the heading tags and Heading 6, the <h6> tag, has the smallest. In fact, you usually only see Web page authors use the <h1>–<h3> tags because the remaining tags, <h4>–<h6>, are actually smaller than normal text. Figure 3.4 shows a sample of all the heading tags compared to normal text.

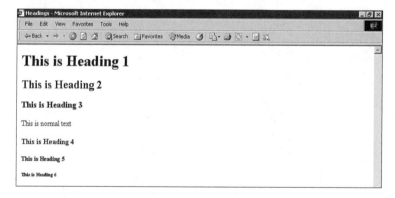

FIGURE 3.4 Notice that HTML's Heading 4 is the same size as normal text, but Headings 5 and 6 are actually smaller.

  Tip Unless you or the people viewing your pages have adjusted the browser's default settings, normal HTML body text appears in 12 point Times New Roman font on most computer systems.

Special Characters

You might find that you sometimes need to use symbols on your Web pages. Symbols (such as +, –, %, and &) are used frequently in our everyday writing, so it's easy to understand that they would appear on a Web page as well. Unfortunately, not all Web browsers display these symbols correctly. HTML uses a little computer shorthand, either using a numerical code or a text code (called an *entity character reference*) to tell the browser how to interpret these symbols. Table 3.1 shows some of the most frequently used codes.

TABLE 3.1   Special Character Codes

Char	Code	Description
&	&amp;	Ampersand
<	&lt;	Less than
>	&gt;	Greater than
©	&copy;	Copyright
®	&reg;	Registered trademark
±	&plusmin;	Plus or minus
^{2}	&sup2;	Superscript 2
^{3}	&sup3;	Superscript 3
´	&acute;	Acute accent
`	&#96;	Grave accent
#	&#35;	Number
%	&#37;	Percent

Appendix C, "Special Characters," contains a more complete list of the characters supported by HTML. You can see how many of these symbols are easy to understand (for example, & for the ampersand and > for the greater than symbol). Some of the characters, such as number and percent, require that you memorize numbered codes. Yuck. The best thing you can do is to make sure that you preview your Web pages in a variety of browsers before publishing them.

 Tip Here's a special character that you should remember: . The symbol stands for *nonbreaking space* and is used to insert a space inside an HTML document. Because HTML ignores extra spaces between words and tags, you'll need to have a way of including extra spaces. You can do that with the   character.

Math and Science Notations

Although HTML was first designed and used by scientists, it has yet to support mathematical and scientific notation with any degree of complexity. HTML does give you two tags to help write simple equations. Together with the codes for special characters, the <sub> (subscript) and <sup> (superscript) tags go a long way toward creating equations, as shown in Table 3.2.

TABLE 3.2 <sup> and <sub> Tags

You Type	The Browser Displays
A² + B² = C²	$A^2 + B^2 = C^2$
CO₂ = Carbon Dioxide	CO_2 = Carbon Dioxide

If you are looking to write more complex equations, you need to be a little more creative. The obvious answer is to write your equation in the program that you usually use, and then use a graphics program to turn it into an image. You can insert that image into any HTML page, as you've already learned. That works, but the solution is limited. Because the equation is graphical, you are not able to index or search for text within the equation. That's a big drawback, but so is the fact that images slow down your page's load time and the fact that your equation cannot be viewed by nongraphical Web browsers.

> **Tip** Some commercial products are available to help you notate mathematical expressions. You can see a list of them on the W3C Web site (www.w3.org/Math/).

English Isn't the Only Language

You can use HTML even if you don't write in English. URLs, hyperlinks, HTML tags, and document formatting elements are language neutral, but text requires a specification all its own. If you write in standard U.S. English, you don't need to make any changes to the way you create your HTML documents. If you are writing text in any other language, however, you should specify the language for the browser. The following HTML samples show the designations for German and French.

```
<html xmlns="http://www.w3.org/1999/xhtml"
      xml:lang="de" lang="de">
```

and

```
<html xmlns="http://www.w3.org/1999/xhtml"
      xml:lang="fr" lang="fr">
```

The language attributes (xml:lang and lang) support the same values as ISO, the International Standards Organization. You can see the full list of supported languages and their codes at www.loc.gov/standards/iso639-2/langcodes.html.

> **Tip** Why is language important? Browsers do not recognize the language you type unless you use the lang attribute. Some search engines use the lang attribute to return only pages written in a specific language. Speech synthesizers use this information to aid in pronunciation. Even some spelling checkers can use the information to recognize misspellings.

Mixing Languages in a Single Page

Although the preceding example shows the `lang` attribute used as part of the `<html>` tag at the top of your document, it's possible that you would want to include text of one language within a document of another language—for example, including a paragraph in French within a document in English. You can assign the `lang` attribute to the `<p>` tag to solve this problem. Look at the following sample:

```
<!DOCTYPE html
    PUBLIC "-//W3C//DTD XHTML 1.0 Transitional//EN"
    "http://www.w3.org/TR/xhtml1/DTD/xhtml1-
    transitional.dtd">
<html xmlns="http://www.w3.org/1999/xhtml"
    xml:lang="en" lang="en">
<head>
<title>Multi-Language Document</title>
</head>
<body>
<p>Put your English text here.</p>
<p lang="fr">Mettez votre texte français ici.</p>
<p lang="en">Put the rest of your English text here.</p>
</body>
</html>
```

Meta Tags

Finally, you get to do something with the `<head>` tag. So far, you've only seen the `<title>` tag used to give information about the document, but you can do a lot more with the `<head>` tag. What's more, aside from the `<title>` tag, information in the `<head>` tag doesn't usually appear in your document. You can use the meta information tag (`<meta>`) to identify the page's author, keywords used for searching, or a brief description to appear in search results. You also can use the `<meta>` tag to give commands to the browser. You can use as many `<meta>` tags as you like in your page. You'll learn how in the sections that follow.

Improved Searching

Search engines (as you'll find in Lesson 17, "Planning for the Future") add the content of your Web pages to their indexes. When a potential visitor enters a search phrase, the search engine checks its index to find that word and returns any pages that include that word. It works great. But, what if you were a realtor and you worked hard at creating a Web page that included the words *houses*, *housing*, *sale*, and *buy*; but didn't include the phrase *real estate*? If that was the phrase your visitor was looking for, they would never find your page. You can use the <meta> tag to include product names, geographic locations, industry terms, and synonyms that people might be searching for. There are three <meta> tags that work to help improve your chances of being found by a search engine:

- **Keywords** Keywords are words that you feel people might use to search for your Web page, or synonyms for words that appear in your document.

- **Description** This is usually a paragraph of information about your page. Some search engines use the information in this tag to summarize your page, but other search engines use the first few lines of text in your actual document.

- **Author** This is your opportunity to shine. Just in case someone is searching for your name, they will find your page if you enter that information into the <meta> tag.

Meta information for search engines comes in pairs: name and contents. The following HTML code includes meta information pairs for each of the preceding <meta> tags.

```
<!DOCTYPE html
    PUBLIC "-//W3C//DTD XHTML 1.0 Transitional//EN"
    "http://www.w3.org/TR/xhtml1/DTD/xhtml1-
    transitional.dtd">
<html xmlns="http://www.w3.org/1999/xhtml"
    xml:lang="en" lang="en">
<head>
<title>Your HTML Page</title>
<meta name="keywords" contents="words that people might
    use to search for your page." />
<meta name="description" contents="a brief paragraph describing
    your document." />
<meta name="author" contents="your name" />
</head>
<body>
```

```
<p>Insert your text here.</p>
</body>
</html>
```

Caution   Remember, <meta> tags only appear in the <head> section of an HTML file.

Refresh and Redirect

There might be times when you want to replace one page with another or want to redirect a link. You might, for example, choose to include a *splash page* on your Web site. You can use the meta information to force the page to change within a given time span using the sample code that follows:

```
<meta http-equiv="refresh" content="time in seconds,
                              URL of the new page" />
```

Splash Page   The introductory page used by some Web page authors to show flashy graphics or a product logo before continuing to the rest of the site's contents.

If you have a page that you update several times a day and you want to make sure that people always see the most recent version, you can enter the page's own URL in the refresh tag. When the browser sees the refresh tag, it presents the requested URL in the specified time.

```
<meta http-equiv="refresh" content="time in seconds,
                              URL for this page" />
```

Caution   Because not all Web browsers support this attribute, authors should include some content on the splash page that enables users to move to the next page on their own.

Expiration Dates

If you have a page that you change frequently, you can specify an expiration date in the <meta> tag to ensure that the Web browser looks for a newer version (rather than displaying an older version, which might still be stored in the browser's memory). Look at the example that follows:

```
<meta http-equiv="expires"
        contents="Wed, 04 December 2006 00:00:00 GMT" />
```

When you enter the URL for this page in your browser, it checks its history files to see whether a copy is stored there. If so, it checks the meta information to see whether this page is still valid. If the expiration date has passed, the browser looks to the Web for a more recent copy before displaying the page.

Table 3.3 reminds you of the formatting tags you learned in this lesson.

TABLE 3.3   HTML Tags Used in This Lesson

HTML Tag	Closing	Description of Use
<b>	</b>	Text appears boldface.
<big>	</big>	Text appears one size larger than normal.
 		Line break. Forces text to the next line.
<em>	</em>	Text appears emphasized (italic). Usually the same as <i>.
<h1>	</h1>	A first-level heading.
<h2>	</h2>	A second-level heading.
<h3>	</h3>	A third-level heading.
<h4>	</h4>	A fourth-level heading. Rarely used.
<h5>	</h5>	A fifth-level heading. Rarely used.
<h6>	</h6>	A sixth-level heading. Rarely used.
<i>	</i>	Text appears emphasized (italic).
<meta />		Identifies information about the document.

HTML Tag	Closing	Description of Use
`<p>`	`</p>`	Paragraph break. Forces a blank line.
`<small>`	`</small>`	Text appears one size smaller than normal.
`<strong>`	`</strong>`	Text appears boldface. Same as `<b>`.
`<sub>`	`</sub>`	Text appears in subscript.
`<sup>`	`</sup>`	Text appears in superscript.
`<tt>`	`</tt>`	Text appears monospaced, as if typed.

In this lesson, you've learned:

- The `<p>` tag, or paragraph tag, tells the browser to add a blank line before it displays any text that follows. The `<br />` tag moves your text to the next line without adding a blank line.

- HTML enables you to add emphasis to your text with several predefined formatting tags.

- Symbols such as +, −, and % require a little computer shorthand to tell the browser how to interpret these symbols. This shorthand begins with an ampersand (&) and ends with a semicolon (;). A more complete list can be found in Appendix C.

- You can add other languages to your HTML documents by using the `lang` attribute on the `<html>` tag.

- Meta information for search engines comes in pairs: `name` and `contents`, and the `<meta />` tags always appear between the `<head>` tags.

LESSON 4

Linking Text and Documents

In this lesson, you will learn how to use HTML's most valuable feature: hyperlinks.

What Is a URL?

Ask anyone and they'll tell you that (far and away) the feature that makes HTML so worthwhile is the ability to *hyperlink* from one place to another. All Web pages, Internet resources, files, and so on, have an address. That address is known as a *Uniform Resource Locator*, or *URL*. Before you can link to another page (or resource), you have to know its address. You can find the URL for any resource in the Address box (or Location box) of your browser.

Hyperlink   The text that enables you to jump from a Web document to another location.

Caution   Although *URL* is the commonly accepted term to describe the location of Internet resources, a new term, *URI* (*Uniform Resource Identifier*), will likely replace it as XML becomes the standard. You'll find out more about XML in Lesson 17, "Planning for the Future."

The <a> tag (called an *anchor*) is used to define hyperlinks. Unlike most other HTML tags, the <a> tag *requires* an attribute. When you use the <a> tag, you must specify whether you want the enclosed text to link *to* someplace (with the `<a href="the URL you want to link to">` tag) or be linked *from* someplace (with the `<a name="the place in a document you want to link to" id="the place in a document you want to link to">` tag). The following section provides some examples.

Hyperlinks

The easiest link to learn is the hyperlink to another location. The `<a>` tag with the `href` attribute and its closing tag, `</a>`, surround any text that you want to highlight. The default hyperlink highlighting in HTML is underlined blue text. In the following example, you would click on the words `click here` to jump (hyperlink) to the document found at the URL inside the quotes (`http://www.microsoft.com`).

```
Please <a href="http://www.microsoft.com">click here</a> to
open the Microsoft Web site.
```

 Tip Did you know that you can copy the URL of any Web page from your browser? Just highlight the address in the Address box (or Location box) and select Edit, Copy (or press Ctrl+C). Then, select Edit, Paste (or press Ctrl+V) to paste the address between the quotes of the `href` attribute.

Linking to Other Files and Email

You can link to more than just other people's Web sites. You can use the same `href` attribute to link to email addresses for other pages of your own Web site, or even to other files on your own computer. The hyperlink to point to another file (second.htm) on *my* own computer, for example, is shown in the following code. In this example, the second.htm file is stored in the same directory as the page linking to it.

```
Please <a href="second.htm">click here</a> to open
    my second Web page.
```

If, however, my second.htm file was stored in another directory (for example, the Links directory), the hyperlink would need to include the directory name too, as in the following:

```
Please <a href="links/second.htm">click here</a> to open
    my other page.
```

Tip   Did you know that you can force your hyperlink to open a new browser window? This is especially handy if you want to link to someone else's Web site without directing traffic away from your own site. Use the `target="_blank"` attribute, as in the following example. Try it!

```
<a href="http://www.somewhere.com/page.htm"
target="_blank">
    Click here</a> to open a related Web site.
```

The `href` attribute changes slightly if you want to link to a file that is not part of your Web site. You need to tell the Web browser that the file is not located on the Web server. You can see how that is accomplished in the following example:

```
<a href="file:\\servername\foldername\filename.extension">
    Click here</a> to open my favorite file.
```

If I want to link to my dogs.doc file in the 4legs folder of my animals server, for example, my hyperlink looks like the following:

```
<a href="file:\\animals\4legs\dogs.doc">click here</a>
    to open my favorite file.
```

Caution   Did you notice that the direction of my slashes changes when I change my link type from `http://` to `file:\\`? The forward slash (/) is always used to separate directory folders on a Web file server. The backslash (\) is used to separate directory folders in Windows and DOS.

You also can link to an email address by using the `mailto` prefix, as shown in the following code line. When you click on the words `click`

here, an email window that enables you to type your message to Mickey
Mouse appears.

```
<a href="mailto:mickey.mouse@disney.com">Click here</a>
   to send mail to Mickey.
```

Linking Within the Same Page

Now that you know how to link to other resources, you might want your
hyperlinks to be more meaningful. HTML enables you to use hyperlinks to
point to a specific spot (or anchor) in an HTML document, instead of just
pointing to the entire document. As an example, suppose that you have a
list of headlines at the top of your HTML document that points to a more
complete article at the bottom of your document. This is easy in HTML.
Remember that anchor tags come with three attributes: href (which has
already been discussed), and name and id (which always appear together).

Anchor   A named point on a Web page. The same
tag is used to create hyperlinks and anchors.

Caution   In the new XHTML and XML standards
(which will eventually replace HTML), the W3C is call-
ing for the use of a new attribute for the <a> tag
(called id) to replace the name attribute. The smart
thing to do (to make sure that you comply with the
new standard when it is released) is to use both attributes in your documents. To avoid problems, use the
same value for both attributes, for example, if
name="dogs" then id="dogs" as well.

The <a> tag also enables you to name an anchor (or bookmark) in your
document with the name and id attributes. HTML then enables you to use
the anchor tag to point directly to that bookmark. Figure 4.1 demonstrates
how the example in the previous paragraph might look in HTML. Figure
4.2 shows that same document in the browser.

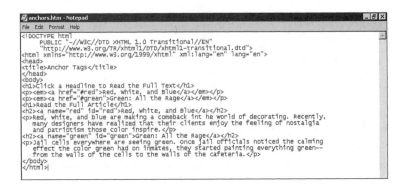

FIGURE 4.1   Notice how the href attribute points to the location named by the name and id attributes.

Caution   The `<a href>` tag includes the same URL format you've seen before, but also includes the # symbol to separate the filename from the named anchor.

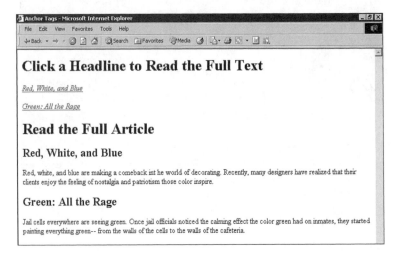

FIGURE 4.2   The `<a>` tag with the href attribute is highlighted, but the `<a>` tag with the name and id attributes is not.

Linking to an Anchor in Another Page

Creating a hyperlink to an anchor in another page requires only one more element: the URL. As you learned before, you can link to an anchor in a file on your own Web site, as shown in Figure 4.3, or you can link to a known anchor in a file on another Web site. The keyword in that sentence is *known*. You can't link to a specific spot on a file unless that spot is already recognized by the Web browser as a named anchor.

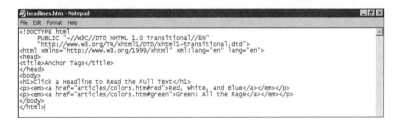

FIGURE 4.3 Notice that each href attribute includes a folder name (articles), a filename (colors.htm), and the specific anchor name (red).

Table 4.1 lists the HTML tags that were discussed in this lesson.

TABLE 4.1   HTML Tags Used in This Lesson

HTML Tag	Closing	Description of Use
`<a href="...">`	`</a>`	Surrounds text that links to another location.
`<a name="...">`	`</a>`	Surrounds text that is linked to.
`<a id="...">`	`</a>`	Same as `<a name>`, but might soon replace it. Use them together as: `<a name="..." id="...">`.

In this lesson, you've learned:

- Anchor tags come with three attributes: `href` (which links *to* someplace), and `name` and `id` (which link *from* someplace).

- You can copy the URL of any Web page from your browser and paste it between the quotes of the `href` attribute in your <a> tag.

- The same `href` attribute links to email addresses, to other pages of your own Web site, or even to other files on your own computer.

LESSON 5
Adding Your Own Style

In this lesson, you will learn how to create style sheets, apply them to your HTML pages, and wow your audience with your creativity.

Style Sheets

As you've already learned, HTML was written as a markup language for defining the structure of a document (paragraphs, headings, tables, and so on). Although it was never intended to become a desktop publishing tool, it does include some basic formatting attributes, such as `bgcolor`, `font-size`, and `align`. In 1996, the W3C first recommended the idea of Cascading Style Sheets (CSS) to format HTML documents. The recommendation, which was updated in mid-1998, enables Web developers to separate the structure and format of their documents.

 Style Sheet A set of rules that determine how the styles are applied to the HTML tags in your documents.

The CSS recommendation describes the following three types of style sheets:

- **Embedded** The style properties are included (within the `<style>` tags) at the top of the HTML document. A style assigned to a particular tag applies to all those tags in this type of document. In this book, you'll see embedded style sheets most often.

- **Inline**   The style properties are included throughout the HTML page. Each HTML tag receives its own style attributes as they occur in the page.

- **Linked**   The style properties are stored in a separate file. That file can be linked to any HTML document using a `<link>` tag placed within the `<head>` tags.

In the following sections, you'll learn how to construct these style sheets and how to apply them to your documents.

Tip   Even without all the formatting benefits that style sheets provide, Web developers can rejoice in knowing that using style sheets will no doubt be the biggest timesaver they've ever encountered. Because you can apply style sheets to as many HTML documents as you like, making changes takes a matter of minutes rather than days.

Before the advent of style sheets, if you wanted to change the appearance of a particular tag in your Web site, you would have to open each document, find the tag you wanted to change, make the change, save the document, and continue on to the next document. With style sheets, you can change the tag in a single style sheet document and have the changes take effect immediately in all the pages linked to it.

Defining the Rules

Style sheet rules are made up of selectors (the HTML tags that receive the style) and declarations (the style sheet properties and their values). In the following example, the selector is the `body` tag and the declaration is made up of the style property (`background`) and its value (`black`). This example sets the background color for the entire document to black.

```
body {background:black}
```

You can see that, in a style sheet, the HTML tag is not surrounded by brackets as it would be in the HTML document, and the declaration is surrounded by curly braces. Declarations can contain more than one property. The following example also sets the text color for this page to white. Notice that the two properties are separated by a semicolon.

```
body {background:black; color:white}
```

You can format this style rule in a number of ways to make it easier to read. For example, the following rule produces exactly the same results as the preceding style:

```
body {background:black;
     color:white}
```

So does this:

```
body {
     background:black;
     color:white
     }
```

If you want to apply the same rules to several HTML tags, you could group those rules together, as in the following example:

```
body, td, h1 {
               background:black;
               color:white
               }
```

Add a Little class

As the old saying goes, rules are made to be broken. What if you don't want every single h1 heading in your document to be white on a black background? Maybe you want every other h1 heading to be yellow on a white background. Let me introduce you to the class attribute. You can apply this attribute to almost every HTML tag, and it's almost like creating your own tags.

Figure 5.1 shows a fairly standard HTML page that uses an aqua table at the top of the page to hold the navigation links, and places other tabular content in yellow tables throughout the document. You can see the HTML document for that page in Figure 5.2.

FIGURE 5.1   An HTML page that formats two tables differently.

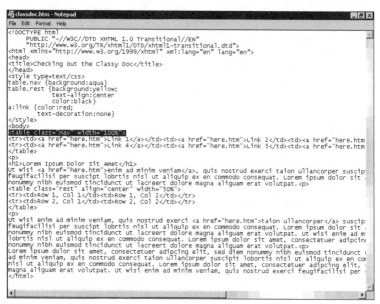

FIGURE 5.2   The HTML document for the page in Figure 5.1.
Notice the `class` attribute in each `<table>` tag.

Take a closer look at the style properties in Figure 5.2. This document defines two `table` styles within the `<style>` tags. The HTML tag name `table` is followed by a period (`.`) and the `class` names (`nav` and `rest`).

```
table.nav {background:aqua}
table.rest {background:yellow;
            text-align:center;
            color:black}
```

When the table is referenced in the body of the document, you must apply the `class` attribute to tell the browser which style properties should be applied. The HTML markup for each table in this example appears in the following HTML code. You can see that the `class` name appears within quotations just like the other HTML attributes (and as with the `width` attribute shown here).

```
<table class="nav" width="100%">
<table class="rest" width=50%>
```

Applying Styles

Before moving on, we'll quickly cover how to apply style properties to your documents. Remember, you have three methods to add style sheets: embedded, linked, and inline. We'll discuss each one in turn.

 Tip In designing your Web site, use linked style sheets to describe your most frequently used styles (the ones that will be formatted in the same fashion for all of the pages in your Web site), such as the heading tags and link tags. Use embedded style sheets to describe the formatting of tags that will remain the same within a single document, or set of documents, such as special table settings or page margins. Use the inline style sheets to describe the formatting of tags that vary from the site-wide formatting applied with the other style sheets, such as for a special callout or sidebar.

Embedded Styles

All the styles are defined at the top of the HTML document within the
<head> tags because they contain information about the entire document.
The styles defined here apply only to the one document in which they
appear. If you plan to use these same styles in another document, you
need to add them there as well.

```
<head>
<style type="text/css">
table.nav {background:aqua}
table.rest {background:yellow;
            text-align:center;
            color:black}
a:link {color:red;
        text-decoration:none}
</style>
</head>
```

Note   The <style> tag almost always includes the
type="text/css" attribute, so you should get used to
adding it.

Linked Styles

Linked style sheets hold all the style properties in a separate file. You then
link the file into each HTML document where you want those style properties to appear.

```
<head>
<link rel="stylesheet" href="mystyles.css" type="text/css">
</head>
```

With this method, I've created a separate file called mystyles.css (for cascading style sheet) that contains all my style properties. You can see that
the same type="text/css" attribute shows up here. Following are the
entire contents of the mystyles.css file. These are the same styles that
showed up in the preceding embedded styles example, but now they
appear in a separate text file.

```
table.nav {background:aqua}
table.rest {background:yellow;
            text-align:center;
            color:black}
a:link {color:red;
        text-decoration:none}
```

> **Tip**   Well-designed Web sites (with more than one
> page) contain repeated page elements and styles. The
> linked style sheet is most appropriate for this type of
> Web authoring. You'll learn more about designing
> effective Web sites in Lesson 13, "Designing with
> HTML."

Inline Styles

With inline styles, the style properties are added to the HTML tag as the
tag is entered. This means that if I want the same style to appear on all
the <h1> tags in my document, I would have to type those styles in all the
<h1> tags. Look at the following example. I am still using the same style
properties, as in the previous examples, but now you can see how the two
tables would be created using inline styles.

```
<table style="background:aqua" width="100%">

<table style="background:yellow; text-align:center;
            color:black" width="100%">
```

Using inline styles, the <style> tag becomes the style attribute. Multiple
style properties are still separated by semicolons, but the entire group of
properties for each tag is grouped within each HTML tag. This type of
style sheet is fine for documents in which you need to apply styles to only
one or two elements, but you wouldn't want to do all that work when you
have a lot of styles to add.

Cascading Precedence

You've got one more thing to learn before moving on. These three styles
are not treated equally by the browsers, nor are they supposed to be.

Web browsers give precedence to the style that appears closest to the tag. So, inline styles (which appear as attributes within the tag itself) are most important. Embedded styles (which appear at the top of the HTML file) are applied next, and linked styles (which appear in another file altogether) are applied last.

Imagine that you have created an embedded style for the <h1> tag, but want to change that style for one occurrence of the <h1> tag in that document. You would create an inline style for that new <h1> tag. The browsers recognize that fact and change the style for that tag to reflect the inline style.

Caution   Style sheet precedence is supposed to place more importance on embedded styles than on linked style sheets. In actual practice, however, you'll find that both Internet Explorer and Netscape treat linked sheets as more important than embedded sheets (but they do treat inline styles as more important than either of the other two). You'll find that you have better luck if you use either linked or embedded styles, but not both.

Formatting Text with Styles

Text is the most important element of any Web page. Without text, there is nothing on the page to help people decide whether it's worth coming back.

Text on an HTML page is structured by the <body>, <p>, <td>, <tr>, <th>, <h1> <h6>, and <li> tags (among others). You can add your own style preferences to each of these tags using the style properties shown in Table 5.1.

Note   Unless you (or the people viewing your pages) have adjusted the browser's default settings, normal HTML body text appears in 12 point Times New Roman font on most computer systems.

In the following example, we've added some embedded style elements
that set the font, font size, and font color for the body text of the basic
HTML document we created in Lesson 2, "Creating Your First Page." In
Figure 5.3, you can see how those styles change the appearance of the
document in the browser.

```
<!DOCTYPE html
      PUBLIC "-//W3C//DTD XHTML 1.0 Transitional//EN"
      "http://www.w3.org/TR/xhtml1/DTD/xhtml1-
transitional.dtd">
<html xmlns="http://www.w3.org/1999/xhtml"
      xml:lang="en" lang="en">
<head>
<title>My First Web Page</title>
<style type="text/css">
body {font-family:"Arial";
      font-size:"12pt";
      color:red}
</style>
</head>
<body>
<p>This is my <b><i>first</i></b> Web page.</p>
</body>
</html>
```

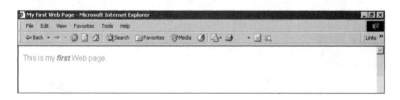

FIGURE 5.3   The browser applies the style attributes to the text in
the <body> tags.

Table 5.1 lists the many style properties that you can use to format your text.

TABLE 5.1   Style Properties for Text

Property	Description of Use and Values
background	Sets the background color for the text.
color	Sets the text color for the text.

continues

TABLE 5.1   Continued

Property	Description of Use and Values
font-family	Sets the font for the text.
font-size	Can be a point size, a percentage of the size of another tag, or xx-small to xx-large.
font-style	normal (which is assumed) or italic.
font-weight	extra-light to extra-bold.
text-align	left, right, center, or justify (full).
text-indent	Can be a fixed length or a percentage.
text-decoration	underline, overline, strikethrough, and none.

Microsoft maintains a brief tutorial for style sheets on its typography site (http://www.microsoft.com/typography/default.mspx). The tutorial teaches Web page authors how style sheets can enhance their documents. The <style> tag for one of those examples is shown in the following code. This is impressive because of the many different styles and classes defined in this document. You can see that you are only limited by your own imagination. You can see the page this style code created in Figure 5.4.

```
<style type="text/css">
body {background: coral}
.copy {color: Black;
    font-size: 11px;
    line-height: 14px;
    font-family: Verdana, Arial, Helvetica, sans-serif}
a:link {text-decoration: none;
    font-size: 20px;
    color: black;
    font-family: Impact, Arial Black, Arial,
                 Helvetica, sans-serif}
.star {color: white;
    font-size: 350px;
    font-family: Arial, Arial, helvetica, sans-serif}
.subhead {color: black;
    font-size: 28px;
    margin-top: 12px;
    margin-left: 20px;
```

```
        line-height: 32px;
        font-family: Impact, Arial Black, Arial,
                     Helvetica, sans-serif}
.what {color: black;
        font-size: 22px;
        margin-left: 20px;
        font-weight: bold;
        font-style: italic;
        font-family: Times New Roman, times, serif}
.quott {color: black;
        font-size: 120px;
        line-height: 120px;
        margin-top: -24px;
        margin-left: -4px;
        font-family: Arial Black, Arial, helvetica, sans-serif}
.quotb {color: black;
        font-size: 120px;
        line-height: 120px;
        margin-right: -1px;
        margin-top: -33px;
        font-family: Arial Black, Arial, helvetica, sans-serif}
.quote {color: red;
        font-size: 24px;
        line-height: 28px;
        margin-top: -153px;
        font-family: Impact, Arial Black, Arial,
                     Helvetica, sans-serif}
.footer {color: cornsilk;
        background: red;
        font-size: 22px;
        margin-left: 20px;
        margin-top: 16px;
        font-family: Impact, Arial Black, Arial,
                     Helvetica, sans-serif}
.headline {color: black;
        font-size: 80px;
        line-height: 90px;
        margin-left: 20px;
        font-family: Impact, Arial Black, Arial,
                     Helvetica, sans-serif}
.mast {color: cornsilk;
        font-size: 90px;
        font-style: italic;
        font-family: Impact, Arial Black, Arial,
                     Helvetica, sans-serif}
</style>
```

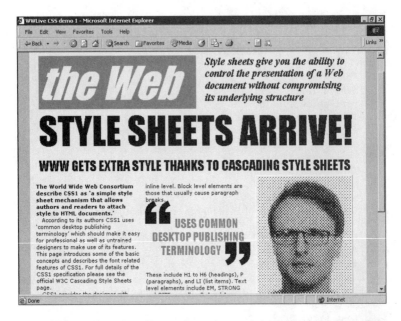

FIGURE 5.4 The preceding style code produced this page, found at
`http://www.microsoft.com/typography/css/gallery/slide3.htm`.

Caution   None of the most popular Web browsers react
the same way to all the style sheet properties. Your best
bet is to remember to test everything before you publish it. Webmaster Stop maintains a table of style sheet
properties mapped to the most popular browsers. Check
out this table (`http://www.webmasterstop.com/118.html`)
to find out whether the style sheet properties you plan
to use are supported by specific browsers.

Link Styles

You have probably seen those bright blue underlined hyperlinks on the Web.
Style sheets have the following selectors to help you change the look of them:

- `a:link`   Sets the styles for unvisited links.

- `a:visited`   Sets the styles for visited links.

- a:active   Sets the styles for the link while it is linking.

- a:hover   Sets the style for the link while your mouse is hovering.

Table 5.2 shows some of the style properties you can assign to your links.

TABLE 5.2   Style Properties for the Anchor Styles

Property	Description of Use and Values
background-color	Sets the background color for the link.
color	Sets the text color for the link.
font-family	Sets the font for the text of the link.
text-decoration	underline, overline, strikethrough, and none.

Tip   One of the most popular style sheet effects on the Web right now is to remove the underlining on hyperlinks. To do this on your pages, just add the text-decoration:none declaration to the a styles, as shown in the following example:

```
a:link {color:yellow;
        text-decoration:none}
```

If you like the look of the underlined hyperlink, you're in luck. You don't have to specify anything at all. Underlining is assumed for all a styles.

Color Styles

As you can see in Table 5.3, you can apply color to your HTML tags in two different ways: with color or with background.

Tip   Check out http://wdvl.internet.com/Graphics/Colour/ for a quick tune-up of Web color selections.

TABLE 5.3   Style Properties for Color

Property	Description of Use and Values
color	Sets the color of the text.
background	Sets the background of the page or text.

Caution   Don't forget to test your pages before you publish them. Not all colors work together. If you've specified a black background color and a black text color, you've got a problem because no one will be able to see your text.

Adding Lines

A horizontal line, or horizontal rule as it is named in HTML, is one of the easiest tags to use. You can insert the <hr /> tag anywhere in your document to insert a horizontal line that extends across the space available.

Take a look at the following sample HTML. It shows three <hr> tags: two used as a section break between text and the other used inside a table cell. Figure 5.5 shows how they appear in the browser.

```
<!DOCTYPE html
    PUBLIC "-//W3C//DTD XHTML 1.0 Transitional//EN"
    "http://www.w3.org/TR/xhtml1/DTD/xhtml1-
transitional.dtd">
<html xmlns="http://www.w3.org/1999/xhtml"
    xml:lang="en" lang="en">
<head>
<title>Horizontal Lines</title>
<style type="text/css">
td {text-align=center}
</style>
</head>
<body>
<p>This is a horizontal line.</p>
<hr />
<p>This is another horizontal line.</p>
<hr />

<table width="50%" rules=cols>
```

```
<tr>
  <td>This is also a<hr />horizontal line.</td>
  <td>There is <br />no line on this<br />side
      of the table.</td>
</tr>
</table>
</body>
</html>
```

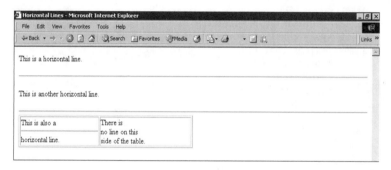

FIGURE 5.5 The `<hr />` tag inserts a horizontal line that stretches across the available horizontal space.

Adding Style to Horizontal Lines

As with other HTML tags, you can use style sheet properties to design your own horizontal rules. You can set the height, width, and color of the line to match the design of your Web page. The following HTML sample shows two different styles attached to the `<hr />` tag. If I use the `hr.red` style, I see a red line that takes up 50% of the horizontal space. If I use the `hr.purple` style, I see a purple line that is 4 pixels high and takes up 75% of the horizontal space.

```
<style type="text/css">
hr.red {color:red;
        width:50%}
hr.purple {color:purple;
           height:4;
           width:75%}
</style>
```

I've used both of those styles in the following sample HTML. Figure 5.6 shows you how those examples look in the browser.

```
<!DOCTYPE html
        PUBLIC "-//W3C//DTD XHTML 1.0 Transitional//EN"
        "http://www.w3.org/TR/xhtml1/DTD/xhtml1-
transitional.dtd">
<html xmlns="http://www.w3.org/1999/xhtml"
        xml:lang="en" lang="en">
<head>
<title>Horizontal Lines</title>
<style type="text/css">
td {text-align=center}
hr.red {color:red;
          width:50%}
hr.purple {color:purple;
              height:4;
              width:75%}
</style>
</head>
<body>
<p>This is a plain horizontal line.</p>
<hr />

<p>This is a purple horizontal line.</p>
<hr class="purple" />

<table width="50%" rules=cols>
  <tr>
    <td>This is a red <hr class="red" />horizontal line.</td>
    <td>There is <br />no line on this<br />
        side of the table.</td>
  </tr>
</table>
</body>
</html>
```

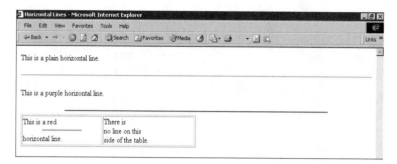

FIGURE 5.6   Applying styles to the `<hr />` tag changes the appearance of the horizontal line.

Margin Styles

Style sheets give you another important advantage: You can specify the margins of almost any HTML element. The margins can be defined in pt, in, cm, or px sizes.

```
body {margin-left: 100px;
      margin-right: 100px;
      margin-top: 50px}
```

You can set the margin-left, margin-right, and margin-top properties individually or combine them into one property called margin that applies the sizes to the top, right, and left margins.

```
body {margin: 100px 100px 50px}
```

The sample CSS document from Microsoft's CSS Gallery (which you looked at earlier) also specifies margins for the text elements. Try it on your documents.

```
<style type="text/css">
body {background: coral }
.subhead { color: black;
    font-size: 28px;
    margin-top: 12px;
    margin-left: 20px;
    line-height: 32px;
    font-family: Impact, Arial Black, Arial,
                 Helvetica, sans-serif}
</style>
```

Tip   Check out the following style sheet references for more help:

- http://webdeveloper.com/html/html_css_1.html **Web Developer's CSS tutorial**

- www.w3.org/TR/REC-CSS2/propidx.html **W3C's list of CSS properties**

- http://www.microsoft.com/typography/ default.mspx **Microsoft's CSS tutorial**

Table 5.4 lists the HTML tags that were discussed in this lesson.

TABLE 5.4   HTML Tags Used in This Lesson

HTML Tag	Closing	Description of Use
<hr />		Creates a horizontal line.
<style>	</style>	Surrounds style sheet properties, or references to external style sheets. The standard open tag should be <style type=_"text/css">.

In this lesson, you've learned:

- The CSS recommendation describes three types of style sheets: embedded, inline, and linked.

- Three different style sheets exist in HTML: embedded, inline, and linked.

- If multiple style sheets are applied to your HTML document, the browser applies the styles of the inline style sheet first, and then the linked style sheets, and then embedded style sheets.

- The <hr /> tag adds a horizontal line to your HTML document. Use style sheet properties to adjust the color, width, and height.

- Remove the underlining on your hyperlinks by adding the text-decoration:none declaration to your a style tags.

Lesson 6
Creating Lists

In this lesson, you will learn to use HTML to organize your text into lists.

Types of Lists

One way to organize the text in your Web pages is with lists. In addition to the obvious benefit of being able to *list* items on a page, they also provide a design benefit by enabling you to break up long pages of ordinary paragraphs. HTML recognizes the following list types and has tags that correspond to each:

- Bulleted (unordered) lists
- Numbered/lettered (ordered) lists
- Definition lists

 Tip You should use ordered lists when the items in the list must be followed in a specific order, and use unordered lists when they do not. You generally use definition lists for terms and their definitions, but they can have other uses as well.

Bulleted (Unordered) Lists

A bullet (usually a solid circle) appears in front of each item in an unordered list. HTML automatically creates the bullet when you use the unordered list tag (`<ul>`) together with the list item tag (`<li>`). Although the following sample HTML shows each list item as a single line of text, your list items can be as long as you want:

```
<ul><li>first item in the list</li>
<li>second item in the list</li>
<li>third item in the list</li></ul>
```

Figure 6.1 shows how the Web browser displays an ordered and an unordered list. The figure includes list examples from many of the following sections. When your list items are longer than a single line of text, the Web browser indents the second line (and any following lines) so that the text lines up.

FIGURE 6.1   Ordered and unordered lists shown in the Web browser.

Formatting Bulleted Lists

HTML automatically adds a solid circle in front of each list item as a bullet, but you have two other choices. Using style sheet tags (which you learned about in Lesson 5, "Adding Your Own Style"), you can select one of two other bullet types: a square or a hollow circle. You can see how your HTML document would look if you chose to use a square bullet instead of the standard solid circle. Figure 6.1 shows how the Web browser displays this bullet type.

```
<!DOCTYPE html
     PUBLIC "-//W3C//DTD XHTML 1.0 Transitional//EN"
     "http://www.w3.org/TR/xhtml1/DTD/xhtml1-
transitional.dtd">
<html xmlns="http://www.w3.org/1999/xhtml"
     xml:lang="en" lang="en">

<head>
```

```
<title>Bullet Options</title>
<style type="text/css">
ul.square {list-style-type:square}
ul.image {list-style-
image:url("http://www.xeroxblankmedia.co.uk/graphics/globe.gif")}
</style>
</head>
<body>
<ul class="square">
<li>a list item</li>
<li>another list item</li>
</ul>

<ul class="image">
<li>a list item</li>
<li>another list item</li>
</ul>
</body>
</html>
```

You'll notice that this sample HTML also includes a style (`list-style-image`). This style enables you to replace the plain HTML bullets with your own image. In this example, I replaced the bullets with an image of a globe. Try changing the URL for one of your own images. You can see the globe image I chose in Figure 6.1.

Numbered (Ordered) Lists

If the items in your list should follow a specific order, as in recipes or instructions, you want to use the ordered list tag (`<ol>`). With this tag, HTML automatically numbers or letters your items for you. Here's an example:

```
<ol><li>first item in the list</li>
<li>second item in the list</li>
<li>third item in the list</li></ol>
```

Notice how similar the two list samples are. Both the `<ul>` and `<ol>` tags call for the individual list items to be identified with the `<li>` tag. Like the `<ul>` tag, HTML has an automatic style for the list items within the `<ol>` tag. HTML automatically numbers the items with the familiar Arabic numerals (1, 2, 3, and so on). What's more, it automatically renumbers the list items if you decide to add or delete items later. Once again, Figure 6.1 has an example of this type of list.

Formatting Numbered Lists

You can use style sheets for formatting ordered lists. In addition to the standard Arabic numerals, there are four other styles that can be applied to your ordered list. Table 6.1 describes each of those types, and the following sample HTML shows how you can use style sheets to create a list ordered by lowercase roman numerals. Figure 6.1 shows an example of such a list in the Web browser.

```
<!DOCTYPE html
     PUBLIC "-//W3C//DTD XHTML 1.0 Transitional//EN"
     "http://www.w3.org/TR/xhtml1/DTD/xhtml1-
transitional.dtd">
<html xmlns="http://www.w3.org/1999/xhtml"
     xml:lang="en" lang="en">
<head>
<title>Bullet Options</title>
<style type="text/css">
ol.lwroman {list-style-type:lower-roman}
</style>
</head>
<body>
<ol class="lwroman">
<li>a list item</li>
<li>another list item</li>
</ol>
</body>
</html>
```

TABLE 6.1 List Style Types

Sample	Style Syntax	Definition
a, b, c	lower-alpha	Lowercase letters
A, B, C	upper-alpha	Uppercase letters
i, ii, iii	lower-roman	Small roman numerals
I, II, III	upper-roman	Large roman numerals

Setting a Start Value

There might be times when you'd like to start an ordered list with a number other than one. Many times when writing instructions, you need to interrupt a numbered list with some other material (such as text or examples), and then continue with the numbered list. To do this in HTML, close the first list, add the additional materials that you need, and then start a new list, using the list item's value attribute to set the beginning number for the new list. Figure 6.2 demonstrates how the following code is interpreted by the browser.

```
<!DOCTYPE html
    PUBLIC "-//W3C//DTD XHTML 1.0 Transitional//EN"
    "http://www.w3.org/TR/xhtml1/DTD/xhtml1-
transitional.dtd">
<html xmlns="http://www.w3.org/1999/xhtml"
    xml:lang="en" lang="en">
<head>
<title>Ordered Lists</title>
<style type="text/css">
</style>
</head>
<body>
<p>It's Payday!</p>
<ol>
<li>Turn in your timecard.</li>
<li>Receive your paycheck.</li>
<li>Endorse your paycheck.</li>
</ol>
<p>Congratulations! You're almost there.</p>
<ol>
<li value="4">Put the check in the bank.</li>
</ol>
</body>
</html>
```

 Caution The value attribute requires that you use Arabic numbering to specify the start value, even if you've chosen roman numerals or letters for your list type.

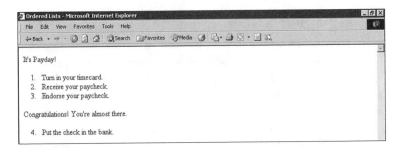

FIGURE 6.2   The Web browser shows an ordered list that was interrupted and started again using the `value` attribute.

Definition Lists

If you need it, HTML has one more type of list available to you: the definition list, which uses the `<dl>` tag. Rather than using the usual `<li>` tag to specify the items in the list, this type of list uses the `<dt>` tag (for definition terms) and the `<dd>` tag for their definitions. Following is an example of the HTML for a definition list, and Figure 6.3 shows how the Web browser formats a definition list.

```
<dl><dt>The Definition Term</dt>
<dd>Is defined below the term.</dd></dl>
```

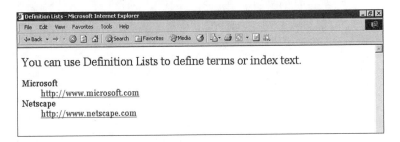

FIGURE 6.3   A definition list displayed in the browser.

Table 6.2 lists the HTML tags that were discussed in this lesson.

TABLE 6.2   HTML Tags Used in This Lesson

HTML Tag	Closing	Description of Use
<dl>	</dl>	Definition list.
<li>	</li>	List item. Used with <ol> and <ul> tags.
<dt>	</dt>	Definition term. The list item of a <dl>.
<dd>	</dd>	Definition data. Describes definition terms.
<ol>	</ol>	Ordered, or numbered/lettered, list.
<ul>	</ul>	Unordered, or bulleted, list.

In this lesson, you've learned:

- HTML recognizes three different list types: unordered (bulleted), ordered (numbered), and definition.

- Rather than the default bullet style (a solid circle), style sheets enable you to select three other bullet types: a square, a hollow circle, or an image of your own.

- The value attribute of the <ol> tag sets the beginning number for your list.

LESSON 7
Creating Tables

In this lesson, you will learn how to build tables using HTML, and how to control the layout and appearance of a Web page using tables.

Simple Tables

Traditionally, *tables* have been used for displaying tabular data (such as numbers) in rows and columns. The flexibility of HTML, however, enables Web developers to create tables that display more than just numbers. In fact, as important as the capability to display tabular data is, even more important to Web designers is the capability to control the layout of other document elements (such as text and images).

Table   An arrangement of horizontal rows and vertical columns. The intersection of a row and a column is called a *cell*.

Caution   Although HTML tables look similar to your favorite spreadsheet, HTML tables don't perform mathematical functions.

HTML tables are not difficult to create, but they do require some organization. All HTML tables begin with the `<table>` tag and end with the `</table>` tag. In between those tags are three other tags to be aware of, as follows:

- `<tr>` defines a horizontal row.

- `<td>` defines a data cell within that row.

- `<th>` specifies a data cell as a table heading. In newer browsers, a table heading cell is formatted as centered and bold.

Remember that Web browsers ignore any spaces, tabs, and blank lines that you include in your HTML document. So, feel free to use spacing to help you keep track of the table tags. Figure 7.1 shows enough blank spaces between the tags so that you can see the rows and columns lining up. It makes it easier to ensure that you don't forget any tags. Figure 7.2 shows how that table looks in a browser.

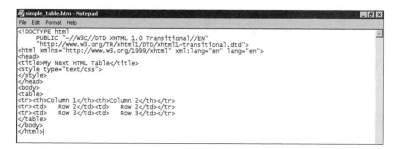

FIGURE 7.1   A simple two-column, three-row HTML table.

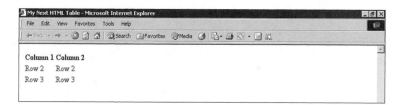

FIGURE 7.2   That same HTML table as it appears in the browser.

Formatting Tables

Now you can add some pizzazz to your simple table. In Table 7.1, you see some of the different style attributes you can apply to HTML tables. Figure 7.3 shows how you can use these attributes to create an HTML table with a little more character. Figure 7.4 shows the way the table appears in a browser.

Tip   The World Wide Web Consortium's Web site (www.w3.org/TR/REC-html40/struct/tables.html) has detailed descriptions of all the attributes available for tables, as well as examples of how you can use them.

TABLE 7.1   Table Style Attributes

Attribute	Default	Use With	Values
align	left	All	Horizontal alignment of cell contents: left, right, center, and char (which aligns around a specific character, usually a decimal or comma).
bgcolor		All	Background color.
border	0	\<table\>	Width of the border (in *pixels*).
cellpadding	0	\<td\>, \<th\>	Space between border and content (in pixels).
cellspacing	0	\<td\>, \<th\>	Space between cells (in pixels).
colspan	1	\<td\>, \<th\>	Number of columns that a cell should span (merge).
rowspan	1	\<td\>, \<th\>	Number of rows that a cell should span (merge).
rules	none	\<table\>	Where the lines (rules) appear between cells: rows, cols, or all.
valign	center	\<td\>, \<tr\>, \<th\>	Vertical alignment of cell contents: top, bottom, or baseline.
width	to fit	All	Width of table or cells (in pixels or as a percentage of the page).

Pixel   A pixel is the size of a single dot of color on your monitor. The monitor's display resolution affects the size of a pixel. A display resolution of 800×600 means that your monitor displays 800 pixels in width by 600 pixels in height. The pixel size on a monitor that displays at a resolution of 1024×800 would be much smaller than one on a monitor with a resolution of 800×600.

A table with a `width` attribute fixed at 800 pixels fills a screen that is set to a resolution of 800×600, but only fills a portion of a screen that is set to 1024×800.

FIGURE 7.3   Table attributes in HTML.

FIGURE 7.4   That same HTML table as it appears in the browser.

Advanced Tables

HTML contains two more attributes that you should be aware of when formatting tables. The colspan (which causes a cell to span two or more columns) and rowspan (which causes a cell to span two or more rows) attributes are invaluable when creating complex tables, although, as you can tell from the HTML in Figure 7.5, using them makes it harder to keep your HTML document organized. Figure 7.6 shows how the table looks in a browser.

```
complex_table.htm - Notepad                                    _ 8 X
File  Edit  Format  Help
<!DOCTYPE html
    PUBLIC "-//W3C//DTD XHTML 1.0 Transitional//EN"
    "http://www.w3.org/TR/xhtml1/DTD/xhtml1-transitional.dtd">
<html xmlns="http://www.w3.org/1999/xhtml" xml:lang="en" lang="en">
<head>
<title>My Next HTML Table</title>
<style type="text/css">
th {background-color:lightblue;
    color:red;
    font-family:Arial}
td {color:blue;
    font-family:Times New Roman}
</style>
</head>
<body>
<table width="100%" borders="1" rules="all">
<tr><th colspan="2">Columns 1 and 2 are combined</th></tr>
<tr><td align="center">  Row 2</td><td rowspan="2">Rows 2 and 3 are combined.</td></tr>
<tr><td align="center">  Row 3</td></tr>
</table>
</body>
</html>
```

FIGURE 7.5   Using the colspan and rowspan attributes to create complex tables.

```
My Next HTML Table - Microsoft Internet Explorer              _ 8 X
File  Edit  View  Favorites  Tools  Help
Back  →   ⊗ ⊠ ⌂  Search  Favorites  Media  ⊘  ⊡· ⊜ ⊗ · ⊠ ⊠

        Columns 1 and 2 are combined
      Row 2
                  Rows 2 and 3 are combined.
      Row 3
```

FIGURE 7.6   That same HTML table as it appears in the browser.

Using Tables for Layout

Look at the source code for some of your favorite Web pages and I bet that you'll find they were created using tables. Following are some of my favorite Web pages that use tables to control the page layout:

- www.ibm.com/us/   The columns of search categories are created with tables.

- www.cnn.com/   This site is essentially a three column table.

- www.microsoft.com/office/editions/prodinfo/default.mspx Microsoft, too, uses tables to design the layout of its Web site.

- www.idolonfox.com/   The *Americal Idol* Web site demonstrates another creative use of tables in layout.

 Tip   Even if you don't plan to place a border around the cells in your table, it's much easier to see how your HTML commands are interpreted by your Web browser when you have the borders turned on (`<table border="1">`). After you are satisfied that the table is formatted correctly and your content is where you want it to be, you can remove the `border` attribute, leaving just the `<table>` tag.

Table 7.2 lists the HTML tags that were discussed in this lesson.

TABLE 7.2   HTML Tags Used in This Lesson

HTML Tag	Closing	Description of Use
`<table>`	`</table>`	Identifies the beginning and ending of a table. All table content must be contained within this tag.
`<td>`	`</td>`	Table data cell. Similar to a column.
`<th>`	`</th>`	Table heading.
`<tr>`	`</tr>`	Table row. Surrounds table cells (`<td>`) and headings (`<th>`).

In this lesson, you've learned:

- Tables can control the layout of HTML document elements (such as text, navigation, and images).

- Extra spaces in your HTML documents help you keep track of the table tags. Web browsers ignore any extra spaces.

- The `colspan` and `rowspan` attributes merge cells so that you can create complex tables.

LESSON 8
Using Graphics

In this lesson, you'll learn how to add pizzazz to your Web pages with graphic images.

Adding Images

If the Web were nothing but text, it would still be technologically impressive, but it wouldn't be nearly as much fun. Adding images to your pages is easy; adding images that make your Web pages look professional just takes a little know-how. Luckily, you'll learn that here—and it shouldn't take longer than 10 minutes.

The two most frequently used graphics file formats found on the Web are GIF and JPEG. The *Joint Photographic Experts Group (JPEG)* format is used primarily for realistic, photographic-quality images. The *Graphics Interface Format (GIF)* is used for almost everything else. One new file format is gaining popularity among designers and will soon be making its presence known: The *Portable Network Graphics* format *(PNG)* is expected to replace the GIF format someday. Don't rush out to replace all your graphics, however; not all browsers support it fully yet.

Tip Sound like a pro—learn how to pronounce the graphic formats you use. GIF is pronounced "jif" (like the peanut butter), JPEG is pronounced "jay-peg," and PNG is pronounced "ping."

Let's get down to business. You add all images by using a single HTML tag, the image source tag, `<img src="location" />`. By now you probably recognize that this tag is actually an `<img />` tag with an attribute (src) and attribute value (*location*), but because all images require a src attribute, it's easier to refer to it as a single tag. You'll also notice that the image tag does not have a corresponding closing tag. It is a single tag and you'll need to remember to add the closing slash at the end: <img />. The result of the following sample HTML appears in Figure 8.1.

```
<!DOCTYPE html
    PUBLIC "-//W3C//DTD XHTML 1.0 Transitional//EN"
    "http://www.w3.org/TR/xhtml1/DTD/xhtml1-
    transitional.dtd">
<html xmlns="http://www.w3.org/1999/xhtml" xml:lang="en"
    lang="en">
<head>
<title>First Images</title>
<style type="text/css">
</style>
</head>
<body>
<p>This is an image in my first Web page.</p>
<img src="http://www.thingstobehappyabout.com/face2.gif" />
</body>
</html>
```

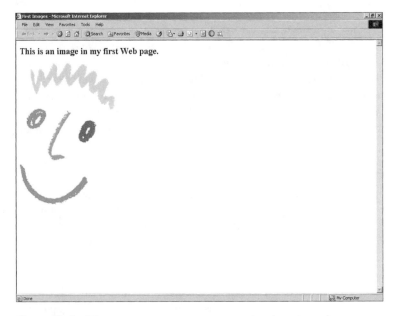

FIGURE 8.1   The <img src="location" /> tag inserts an image into your HTML document.

Caution Be aware that the World Wide Web Consortium, the standards-setting body for HTML, is considering replacing the `<img />` tag with the more generic `<object>` tag. To add an image using the `<object>` tag, follow this format:

```
<object data="location" type="image/gif"> text
    describing the image... </object>
```

Adding Alternate Text

When browsing the Web, you might have noticed that many times when you move your mouse pointer over an image, you see a text pop-up that describes the image, or tells you something more about the area of the Web site that image represents. You can see an example of that type of text pop-up in Figure 8.2.

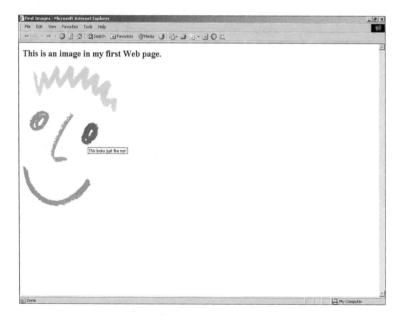

FIGURE 8.2 The `alt` attribute adds a text pop-up to your image.

The following HTML sample shows how the `alt` attribute is added into the `<img />` tag. Like the `src` attribute, the `alt` attribute tells the browser more information about the `image`. And, like the `src` attribute, you should always use the `alt` attribute with the `<img />` tag.

```
<img src="http://www.thingstobehappyabout.com/face2.gif"
 alt="This looks just like me!"/>
```

 alt attribute   Sets the *alternate text* for a graphic. It was named `alt` because it describes the text some people would see as an alternative to the image that others would see.

The `alt` attribute has another very important purpose. Many people with slower modem connections to the Web decide to customize their browser settings to ignore graphics because loading graphics into a Web browser can sometimes take a long time. Remember, too, that not all browsers enable you to view graphics. Some browsers, such as Lynx, have no graphics capabilities at all. The `alt` attribute ensures that people who can't view your graphics can still understand their context.

 Caution   Although you should use the `alt` attribute whenever you use the `<img />` tag, make sure that you don't specify irrelevant text. For example, there is no point in specifying alternate text for a decorative image (such as a bullet or a line); instead, specify an empty value (`alt=" "`).

Without any other attributes, the browser displays the image at its original size and aligns the bottom of the graphic with the bottom of the text. You can adjust both those settings using style sheet tags.

Image Attributes

You can use other attributes of the `<img />` tag to change the image size.
Table 8.1 shows some of these attributes, and the following sections provide some examples for adding these attributes to your documents.

TABLE 8.1 Attributes Used with the `<img />` Tag

Attribute	Values	Description of Use
height	Pixel or percent	Specifies the height of an image.
width	Pixel or percent	Specifies the width of an image.

Adjusting the Height and Width

You can adjust the size of your image using the `height` and `width` attributes. You can set these attributes to a fixed pixel size or a percentage of the page size. Look at the following sample HTML lines. The first line sets the happy face image from Figure 8.1 to a fixed pixel size of 60 pixels high and 60 pixels wide. The second line sets the same image to 6% of the page width and 10% of the page height. Figure 8.3 shows how both of these look in the browser.

```
<img src="http://www.thingstobehappyabout.com/face2.gif"
 alt="This looks just like me!" height="60" width="60" />
<img src="http://www.thingstobehappyabout.com/face2.gif"
 alt="This looks just like me!" height="10%" width="6%" />
```

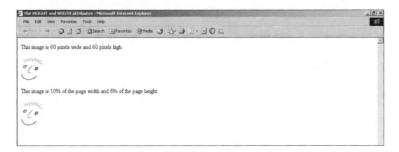

FIGURE 8.3 The `height` and `width` attributes control the size of the image.

The Web browser interprets pixels and percentages equally well when rendering an image. You need to remember, however, that your Web visitors may not use the same monitor display settings that you do. What does this mean to you? My monitor is set to 800 pixels wide. In the preceding HTML sample, I set the happy face image to 6% of the page width, or 48 pixels wide. If I viewed the same page on a monitor set to 1024 pixels wide, that same 6% of the page width would now equal 61 pixels, which is much wider than I wanted.

If you truly want the image to be a certain percentage of the page (as you might for a graphical line), then use percentages. Using percentages ensures that the image will take up the space you want it to. If you want the image to appear a specific size, use the pixel setting.

Caution   Be sure to change both the height and width of your image if you plan to resize them. Adjusting only one of them will stretch the image out of proportion. An alternative is to resize the image in your image editor.

Tip   Create the illusion of faster image loading. Regardless of whether you're resizing an image or not, you should always include the `height` and `width` attributes because they give the browser important information about how much space will be required to show the image on the page. This way, the browser can set that space aside and continue building other aspects of the page even while the image downloads. This gives the impression that the page loads faster since the viewer doesn't have to wait for the entire image to download before looking at other areas of the page.

Aligning Text and Images

You can use the `align` attribute of the `<img />` tag to force an image to appear on the left or right of a section of text. You can see an example of this attribute in action in Figure 8.4.

```
<img src="http://www.thingstobehappyabout.com/face2.gif"
  alt="This looks just like me!" height="60" width="60"
  align="right" />
```

You also can use the `align` attribute to vertically align an image with the text. The `align` attribute has three more values: `top`, `bottom`, and `center`, which are discussed in the following list. Figure 8.4 shows you a sample HTML document using the vertical alignment properties.

- Setting the `align` attribute to `top` aligns the top of the image with the top of any surrounding text.

- Setting the `align` attribute to `bottom` aligns the bottom of the image with the bottom of any surrounding text.

- Setting the `align` attribute to `center` aligns the center of the image with the center of any surrounding text.

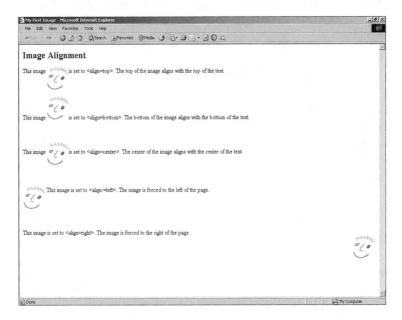

FIGURE 8.4 Notice how the `align` attribute forces the image to align with the text.

Caution Be sure to preview your HTML documents in the browser (or in several browsers) to make sure that you are happy with how they look before you publish them. Not all browsers treat these align attributes in the same way.

Using Images as Links

Images are good for more than just looks. You can use them to provide creative hyperlinks to other documents. HTML makes this easy because using an image as a link is exactly the same as using text. You are still using the anchor tag (the <a> tag you learned about in Lesson 4, "Linking Text and Documents") to surround the item you want to act as the hyperlink to another document. When you link from an image, the anchor tags must surround the image tag. Following is an example of the HTML you would use:

```
<a href="DOC2.htm">
<img src="http://www.thingstobehappyabout.com/face2.gif"
   alt="This looks just like me!"  height="60" width="60" />
</a>
```

When your visitors move their mouse pointers over the face image in this sample, they will see a pop-up that says, "This looks just like me!" When the visitors click on the image, they will open the DOC2.htm file referenced by the anchor tag.

Thumbnail Images

Another popular use of the hyperlinking capability of HTML is to link from one image to another. Why would you want to do that? Well, many times the image you want to display is so large that it takes longer to load into the browser than you think people would like to wait. If that's so, you can create a smaller version of the file, called a *thumbnail*, that will load more quickly into the browser. The visitor simply clicks the thumbnail if he wants to open the larger file. Here's how it's done.

```
<a href="large_image.jpg">
<img src="thumbnail.jpg" alt="Click here to view a larger
  image." height="60" width="60" />
</a>
```

As you can see, clicking the thumbnail.jpg image will open another image (large_image.jpg). The `alt` attribute in this sample tells the visitor how to open the larger image.

Tip   Many image editor programs provide tools to help you create thumbnail images of your large graphics. You can also use standalone products, such as Cerious Software's Thumbs Plus available for download at `ftp://ftp.cerious.com/pub/cerious/` `thmpls32.exe`.

Image Etiquette

Images are fun and colorful and easy to add to your HTML, but following are some etiquette rules to follow if you want your visitors to be happy with your site.

- The larger an image's file size, the longer it will take to load into the browser. Because most visitors to the World Wide Web still use a slow speed modem to connect from home, their time is precious. If you remember that and make sure to use small images whenever possible, you'll find that your visitors are happier.

- Not only is the file size of the individual image important, but also is the total file size of your HTML document. The more images you add—even small images—the larger your file size will become. Previewing your page in several browsers will help you determine how long your page will take to load in the browser. If you find the time too slow, so will your visitors.

- While the `alt` attribute is one of the most important attributes (because it should be used every time you use the `<img />` tag), it pays to remember a simple guideline: Make sure that the text for the `alt` attribute is relevant to the image—anything less will frustrate your visitors.

- On the subject of relevance: Be sure that your images are relevant to the text. An image of an airplane works great if you're talking about travel plans, but means nothing if you're talking about wildlife.

- You can find images all over the Internet, and saving them to your own computer for use later is easy (see the following Tip). Just as in the publishing world, however, graphic designers can protect their images by copyright. If you've found an image you like on a commercial Web site, look for a copyright notice or other legal statement that indicates whether the image is free for the taking. There are plenty of free images available on the Internet without using copyrighted material.

 Tip   You can copy any Web image to your own computer, as long as it isn't protected by copyright. Just right-click on the image (or hold down the mouse button if you are on a Macintosh computer) and select Save Image As from the pop-up menu. Save the file on your own computer and use it as you would any other image file.

Table 8.2 lists the HTML tags that were discussed in this lesson.

TABLE 8.2   HTML Tags Used in This Lesson

HTML Tag	Closing	Description of Use
`<img src="location" />`		Adds an image to an HTML document.
`<object>`	`</object>`	Adds an object (can be used for images) to a HTML document.

In this lesson, you've learned:

- The two most frequently used graphics file formats found on the Web are GIF and JPEG. JPEG is used primarily for realistic, photographic-quality images; GIF is used for almost everything else. PNG is expected replace GIF sometime in the future.

- All images are added to HTML documents with the image tag and the source attribute, `<img src="location" />`.

- You can use the `<a>` tag to link an image to another document.

- Images are part of the fun of Web pages, but they are also part of the problem; larger file sizes mean longer page load times.

LESSON 9
Mapping Images

In this lesson, you'll learn how to use image maps to link one image to many pages.

What Are Image Maps?

You've learned how to use an image to link to another page, but did you know that you can subdivide a single image and link each part of that image to another page? This type of subdivided image is called an *image map*.

 Image Map   An image that is divided into pieces that are linked to (or, mapped to) more than one resource, such as an HTML page, a file, or another image.

You've probably seen image maps on the Web, even if you didn't know what they were. Rather than creating a different image for each button in the navigation bar, many Web designers create a single image that contains all the buttons and then use image maps to link each button to the appropriate page. Figure 9.1 shows one example of such a navigation bar. Look at the following additional examples:

- The Amazon Web site (http://www.amazon.com) also uses image maps in its navigation bar.

- The map on the Travel Alberta Web site (http://www1.travelalberta.com/content/maps/) uses an image map to direct visitors to information about specific regions of the province.

- The Johnson's Baby Soft Web site (http://johnsons babysoft.com/) uses an image map to link to specific product information for the products shown on its home page.

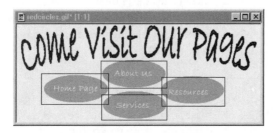

FIGURE 9.1 This image has been subdivided into four parts (one for each button on my navigation bar). Notice that some pieces of the image will not be linked to anything. Do not draw the boxes on your own image; I included them for demonstration purposes.

Finding the Coordinates

Like any other map, image maps have coordinates. In an image map, the coordinates, which are written as pixels, mark the corners of the piece of the image that will be linked to a specific URL. Before you can create any image map, you have to know the coordinates for your image.

Many image editors are available that can help you determine these coordinates and give them to you in a file so that you can cut and paste them into your HTML document. However, it's a lot easier to let your image editor do the work for you. Just type "create image map" into your favorite Web search engine to find several applications.

 Tip A free trial version of Paint Shop Pro can be downloaded from the Corel® Web site at http://www.corel.com/servlet/Satellite? pagename=Corel3/Trials/DownloadContainer.

If you want to create your own image map, use the image editor to find the coordinates, write them down, and add those coordinates to your HTML file. Figure 9.2 shows you how Paint Shop Pro displays the coordinates for an image. I highlighted the portion of my navigation bar that I wanted to map to my home page and Paint Shop Pro told me which coordinates to use. As the figure shows, the highlighted section is a rectangle with corners at 1, 107 and 189, 167.

 Tip   You can divide your image into rectangular, circular, or irregular polygon shapes. The rectangle is the easiest shape to use when you're getting started and that's the shape used in Figure 9.2.

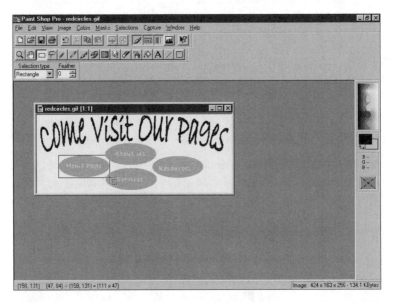

FIGURE 9.2   Paint Shop Pro displays the coordinates of a selected region of the image in the lower-left corner.

Caution   The pixel coordinates for an image mark the corners of the portion of the image you are highlighting. The coordinates are relative to the entire image, not to the position of the image on the Web page. Use your image editor to gather the coordinates and you won't get confused.

Client Side Versus Server Side

With HTML, you can create image maps that work on the client side and the server side. The following list indicates the differences:

- *Client side*   When you click on a client-side image map, the Web browser does all the work to bring you to the new location. The browser selects the link that was specified for the activated region and follows it.

- *Server side*   When you click on a server-side image map, the server that stores the map interprets the commands and brings you to the page to which you are linked.

So how do you know which one to use? Most Web page authors only use client-side image maps because they are faster and anyone with a version 3.0 browser or higher can view them. You can always provide text links for older browsers that don't recognize the client-side image maps. Because client-side image mapping is the type of image map used most often, it is the one you'll learn about in the following section.

 Tip   When you are planning your Web page design, remember that you might not need to use an image map at all. You can place several smaller images close together for the same look. As long as the areas you want to link are primarily rectangular, this process is very easy with HTML and the `<img>` tag you learned in Lesson 8, "Using Graphics."

Creating Client-Side Image Maps

Let's get started. After you have an image and have determined the coordinates for each piece of the image, you can begin mapping your image in HTML. The following HTML sample shows the image map I created for the navigation bar shown in Figure 9.1:

```
<!DOCTYPE html
     PUBLIC "-//W3C//DTD XHTML 1.0 Transitional//EN"
     "http://www.w3.org/TR/xhtml1/DTD/xhtml1-
transitional.dtd">
<html xmlns="http://www.w3.org/1999/xhtml"
     xml:lang="en" lang="en">
<head>
<title>Image Maps</title>
<style type="text/css">
body {text-align="center"}
</style>
</head>
<body>
<map name="NavBar" id="NavBar">
<area shape="rect" coords="270, 91, 416, 138"
     href="resources.htm" alt="resources" " />
<area shape="rect" coords="139, 117, 287, 166"
     href="services.htm" alt="services" "" />
<area shape="rect" coords ="139, 61, 290, 111"
     href="about.htm" alt="about us" />
<area shape="rect" coords ="5, 84, 157, 139"
     href="default.htm" alt="home page" />
</map>
<img src="redcircles.jpg" width="424" height="166"
     alt="My Nav Bar" border="0" usemap="#NavBar" />
</body>
</html>
```

Look at the HTML example for image maps a little closer:

- `<map name="x" id="x">`   Every image map needs a name and an id. It works just like the named anchor tag <a> you saw in Lesson 4, "Linking Text and Documents." It identifies the section of the HTML document that you want to reference from your image.

- `<area shape="w" coords="x" href="y" alt="z" />`   An <area /> tag is required for each portion of an image that will be linked. It identifies the shape of that portion, the coordinates for it, and the URL to which it will lead.

- `</map>`   This tag closes the preceding `<map name>` tag.

- `usemap="#Map Name"`   usemap is an attribute of the `<img />` tag. It points the Web browser to the correct image map for this image. Notice the # sign that precedes the map name; it works just like creating a hyperlink to a named anchor within the current document.

The Web browser sees the image map and knows that the image will be linked. In Figure 9.3, you can see that the mouse pointer changes into a hand when it hovers over a portion of the image that is mapped, as it does when placed over any other hyperlink.

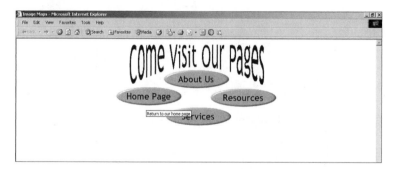

FIGURE 9.3   The image from Figure 9.2 displayed in the Web browser.

Adding Text Links for Older Browsers

Because client-side image maps can be interpreted only by version 3.0 or later Web browsers, you'll need to provide another way for your visitors to get to the other pages in your Web site. The easiest way to do this is to provide text links under your image, as shown in the following HTML sample and in Figure 9.4:

```
<img src="redcircles.jpg" width="424" height="166"
    alt="My Nav Bar" usemap="#NavBar" />
<p align="center" />
<a href="default.htm">Home Page</a> ¦
<a href="about.htm">About Us</a> ¦
<a href="resources.htm">Resources</a> ¦
<a href="services.htm">Services</a>
```

As you can see, text links are standard HTML <a href> links. They will follow the <img /> tag and direct the viewers to the same pages they could reach with the image map. Figure 9.4 shows you how these links will look in the Web browser.

FIGURE 9.4 The image from Figure 9.2 displayed in the Web browser, with additional text links provided for older browsers.

Table 9.1 lists the HTML tags that were discussed in this lesson.

TABLE 9.1 HTML Tags Used in This Lesson

HTML Tag	Closing	Description of Use
<area />		Identifies the shape (circle, rect, or poly), coordinates (in pixels), and URL for each section of the image.
<map name>	</map>	Surrounds the image map and gives a reference name to be used with the usemap="#map name" attribute.

In this lesson, you've learned:

- Image maps link a single image to multiple Internet resources. The most popular examples of image maps on the Web are for navigation bars.

- Paint Shop Pro and other graphics programs enable you to create your image, and determine the coordinates for the image map.

- Image maps can be contained within your HTML document or in a separate file.

LESSON 10
Creating Frames

In this lesson, you'll learn to create frames. You'll also learn why some people don't like them and how you can use them effectively.

Simple Frames

HTML *frames* give you a way to display two or more HTML documents at once. Each frame in the browser window displays its own HTML document. Those documents can link to each other or remain completely separate entities.

 Frame   A complete HTML document that appears inside of, or alongside, one or more other HTML documents within the same browser window.

Most often, as in Figure 10.1, you'll see frames used as a navigation bar on a Web site. The navigation frame can appear on any side of the document, but you'll find it most often on the top or left margins because English (the language of the majority of Web pages) is oriented from top to bottom and left to right.

To create frames, you'll need to create a new type of HTML document, called a frameset. A *frameset* is a special type of HTML document that defines how many frames will be displayed and which HTML documents will appear in each frame. The frameset document for the page is displayed in Figure 10.1.

FIGURE 10.1 A simple two-frame document as it appears in the browser. The left frame contains the site's navigation bar and the right frame contains the pages to which the navigation buttons link.

```
<!DOCTYPE html
       PUBLIC "-//W3C//DTD XHTML 1.0 Frameset//EN"
       "http://www.w3.org/TR/xhtml1/DTD/xhtml1-frameset.dtd">
<html xmlns="http://www.w3.org/1999/xhtml"
       xml:lang="en" lang="en">
<head>
<title>First Frameset</title>
<style type="text/css">
</style>
</head>
<frameset cols="20%,*">
<frame src="toc.htm" name="left" id="left" />
<frame src="latin.htm" name="main" id="main" />
  <noframes>
    <body>
    <p><a href="toc.htm">Table of Contents</a></p>
    </body>
  </noframes>
</frameset>
</html>
```

> **Tip** Did you notice that the <!DOCTYPE> tag changed? In Lesson 2, "Creating Your First Page," you learned that XHTML has three variations. The frameset variation is used whenever you create framed pages.

If you compare this document with a regular HTML document, you should notice right away that the <body> tag is missing. A frameset document uses a new tag, <frameset>, to replace the <body> tag. Within the <frameset> tag, you'll see the <frame /> tag, which is used to describe the contents of each frame, and the <noframes> tag, which is used to instruct the browser what to display in the event the viewer's browser does not support frames, including adding the <body> tag again. Confused? Let's take a closer look at each of these tags.

<frameset>

Within the <frameset> tag, you will need to define the orientation of the frames—in vertical columns, cols, or in horizontal rows, rows. This orientation attribute also requires you to define the size of each of your frames. For example, if you have three vertical frames in your frameset, you will need to specify three size attributes. Look again at the <frameset> tag in the preceding HTML sample.

```
<frameset cols="20%,*">
```

This tag defines two vertical columns. The first column is 20% of the screen width; the second column fills the remainder of the screen—80%. The asterisk (*) tells the browser to fill the remainder of the screen. You can use the same trick if you are defining more than two frames. Although it shows only two values, the following <frameset> tag will actually be used to define *three* horizontal rows. The first row has been set to 20% of the length of the screen; the asterisk forces the browser to equally divide the remainder of the screen between the other two rows.

```
<frameset rows="20%,*">
```

You don't have to let the browser figure out the size of your frames. If you are a perfectionist, you can do your own math and specify the size yourself. Just remember that the total value of the sizes can't be more than 100% of the screen. Now that makes sense, doesn't it?

> **Tip**   You can specify the size of your frames in pixels or as a percentage of the browser window by using the % sign as in the following tag:
>
> `<frameset cols="50%,50%">.`
>
> You don't have to use the % sign, however. You can use a forward slash (/) as an abbreviation of the % sign, as in the following tag:
>
> `<frameset cols="50/,50/">.`

`<frame />`

Like the `<img />` tag you learned about in Lesson 8, "Using Graphics," the `<frame />` tag uses the src (source) attribute to tell the browser where to find the document to display. The important thing to remember when you are setting up your frameset document is that you are defining the start page for your Web site, or the first framed page in your site. You don't have to figure out every possible combination of pages that might appear, you only have to specify the first one.

The `<frame />` tag also requires the name and id attributes. Most people name their frames by their location on the browser window. The `<frame />` tags in the following example, for instance, call the frame that appears on the left of the screen, left, and the other frame main because it will hold the main pages of the Web site.

```
<frame src="toc.htm" name="left" id="left" />
<frame src="latin.htm" name="main" id="main" />
```

> **Tip**   You could name the frames anything (Dog, Cat, Red, or Blue), but you'll find them easier to remember if you stick to something simple.

Following are a few more attributes of the `<frame />` tag that might come in handy:

- `frameborder`   With this attribute, you can remove the small border line that separates the frames. In Figure 10.2, the border has been removed from the sample frameset.

FIGURE 10.2   Figure 10.1 with the frameborder attribute set to "0".

- `marginwidth` or `marginheight`   These attributes specify (in pixels) the space between the border and the text in the frame.

- `scrolling`   Using the values of `yes`, `no`, or `auto`, you can tell the browser whether or not to add a scrollbar next to the frame. Don't worry, however; even if you've specified `scrolling="no"`, the browser will display a scrollbar if the content of the frame exceeds the size of the frame.

- `noresize`   Just like any other window, you can resize frames manually by dragging the frame's border (even when the `frameborder=` `"0"` attribute has been specified). You can prevent that capability by specifying the `noresize` attribute in your frameset.

`<noframes>`

The `<noframes>` tag that appears in the preceding example tells the browser what to do if it doesn't know how to display frames, or if your visitor has adjusted his browser's settings to refuse frames.

```
<noframes>
<body>
<p><a href="toc.htm">Table of Contents</a></p>
</body>
</noframes>
```

The <noframes> tag is not required and many Web page authors choose to ignore it, but it takes very little effort to add it and it makes good sense if you want to be certain that everyone will be able to view your Web site.

While it's true that many authors ignore the <noframes> tag, you'll find that just as many authors choose to create an entire non-framed version of their Web site. I happen to think that's overkill.

If you are using frames as a navigation bar, you could make a couple simple changes to your main HTML pages to help people who can't see the frames navigate your site. In Figure 10.3, I've made the same frameset document from Figure 10.1 work for people who can't see frames. By adding a simple one-row table to hold a duplicate set of navigation elements, someone who stumbles upon your page, but can't see the frame on the left, can still navigate the site.

FIGURE 10.3 Adding a navigation bar to the top of each of the main pages will make this site work for those people who can't view framed pages.

Nested Frames

You might want to be more creative with your frame layout. You can use the
<frameset> tag more than once in a single frameset document. This feature
enables you to nest frames within each other. Following is an example of a
nested frame. I indented the second <frameset> to make it easier to read.

```
<!DOCTYPE html
      PUBLIC "-//W3C//DTD XHTML 1.0 Frameset//EN"
      "http://www.w3.org/TR/xhtml1/DTD/xhtml1-frameset.dtd">
<html xmlns="http://www.w3.org/1999/xhtml"
      xml:lang="en" lang="en">
<head>
<title>First Frameset</title>
<style type="text/css">
</style>
</head>
<frameset rows="15%,*,10%">
<frame src="sitename.htm" name="top" id="top" />
   <frameset cols="20%,*,11%">
     <frame src="toc.htm" name="left" id="left" />
     <frame src="latin.htm" name="main" id="main" />
     <frame src="motto.htm" name="right" id="right" />
   </frameset>
<frame src="contacts.htm" name="bottom" id="bottom" />
   <noframes>
     <body>
     <p><a href="toc.htm">Table of Contents</a></p>
     </body>
   </noframes>
</frameset>
</html>
```

The first <frameset> tag defines three horizontal frames, but the second
<frameset> tag divides the middle row into three column frames. Figure
10.4 shows you how this nested frameset will appear in the browser.

FIGURE 10.4   All the borders have been left showing to help you see where the nested frames are in this example.

<iframe>

You can create a frame one more way by using the <iframe>, or inline frame, tag. Rather than creating a separate frameset document, you define an inline frame within a regular HTML document because it appears in the middle of another document. Figure 10.5 shows the same content as the sample in Figure 10.4, but this page was created using an inline frame. You can see the HTML document for this page in Figure 10.6.

You can apply all the same attributes for regular frames to the <iframe> tag except the noresize attribute because unlike regular frames, inline frames cannot be resized.

Caution   As of right now, the <iframe> tag only works with Internet Explorer 4 and higher browsers, so don't try to use it unless you know your audience has one of those browsers.

FIGURE 10.5 The scrollable document in the center of this page was added with an inline frame.

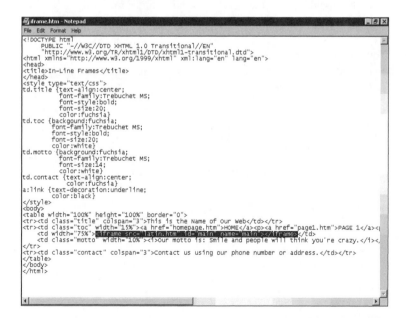

FIGURE 10.6 Style sheet properties are used to help define the colors and fonts for this document. The <iframe> tag is actually embedded inside a table to achieve the page layout shown in Figure 10.5.

Tip Throughout the book, you have been cautioned that not all browsers support all the HTML tags you've learned. For a fee, WebSideStory's StatMarket® tracks browser usage and other fun statistics on its Web site (http://www.websidestory.com/services-solutions/datainsights/statmarket/overview.html). You can use that knowledge to decide whether you are willing to take the risk of using a tag such as `<iframe>`, which is not supported by all browsers.

Linking Between Frames

Think back to Lesson 4, "Linking Text and Documents," when you learned how to create hyperlinks. You'll remember that you can use the `<a name="x" id="x">` tag to name an anchor, or target, within a document that could be linked to directly, as shown in the following code.

```
<a name="PointA" id="PointA">Point A</a>
```

You'll remember that you need to use the anchor tag, `<a href="url#anchor">`, to surround the text that you want to highlight, as shown in the following example:

```
<a href="DOC2.htm#PointA">Click Here to go to Point A</a>
```

All frames also have the `name` and `id` attributes assigned to them. You can use that name to specify which frame you want your hyperlink to open in. Let's look at the HTML code for the toc.htm file used in the preceding examples.

```
<!DOCTYPE html
    PUBLIC "-//W3C//DTD XHTML 1.0 Frameset//EN"
    "http://www.w3.org/TR/xhtml1/DTD/xhtml1-frameset.dtd">
<html xmlns="http://www.w3.org/1999/xhtml"
    xml:lang="en" lang="en">

<head>
<title>Table of Contents</title>
<style type="text/css">
```

```
</style>
</head>
<body>
<p><a href="homepage.htm" target="main">HOME</a></p>
<p><a href="page1.htm" target="main">Page 1</a></p>
<p><a href="page2.htm" target="main">Page 2</a></p>
<p><a href="page3.htm" target="main">Page 3</a></p>
<p><a href="page4.htm" target="main">Page 4</a></p>
</body>
</html>
```

Now you see a new attribute has been attached to the <a href> tag: target. The target attribute refers to the *target frame* for the hyperlink. Besides the frame names that you've specified in your frameset document, you can target the following other three names:

- <a href="*url*" target="blank"> This tag opens the hyperlink in a new browser window.

- <a href="*url*" target="self"> This tag opens the hyperlink in the same window where the hyperlink was. If the hyperlink was in a frame, the link will open in the same frame, replacing that frame document.

- <a href="*url*" target="top"> This tag opens the hyperlink in the same browser window. If the hyperlink was in a frame, the link will open in the same frame, replacing the entire frameset.

Target Frame   The name of the frame in which a hyperlink will open.

Caution   Always specify the target attribute whenever you are working with frames. If you don't specify the target frame, the browser generally will replace the current frame with the target document, which might not be what you'd intended.

The Two Biggest Problems with Frames

Mention frames to any Web site developer, and you'll be sure to get an earful. Good or bad, people always have an opinion. You've already seen how useful they can be at providing navigational information, but let's see why so many people dislike them.

Tip   Jakob Nielsen, one of the Web's most respected usability experts, maintains a Web page called (and pardon my French), Why Frames Suck (Most of the Time), in which he discusses some of the many problems users have with frames. You can read his original 1996 article at www.useit.com/alertbox/9612.html, which was later updated in 1999 (http://www.useit.com/alertbox/990502.html). Though not a recent article, the concerns he raises are still valid today.

So Many Pages, So Few URLs

When you load your frameset document into your browser, you are telling the browser to load all the pages into this same document, following the selected hyperlinks. So? Take a look at the URL for your frameset document. My URL is C:\Webshare\wwwroot\sams\frame2.htm. No matter how many times I click the hyperlinks in my framed pages, the URL stays the same because all those framed pages are loading into the same frameset document.

Why is that a problem? Suppose that my best customer is browsing my site and she is looking at the *wonderful* information on Page4.htm. She decides to save the URL in her Favorites (or bookmark it) so that she doesn't have to search for the information again. The URL she saves is C:\Webshare\wwwroot\sams\frame2.htm, not C:\Webshare\wwwroot\sams\page4.htm, which is what she was actually looking at. There is no guarantee that when she opens that URL in the browser, it will open on Page4.htm, as she wanted in the first place. How frustrating!

If you right-click the mouse (or hold the mouse button if you have a Macintosh), you can click Properties in the shortcut menu. On the Properties dialog box is the URL for that particular page (see Figure 10.7). You can highlight and copy that URL into the Address field of your browser to open later. When you do this, however, you will not see the framed version of the site; you will only see the single document that you saved, with no additional navigation to help you.

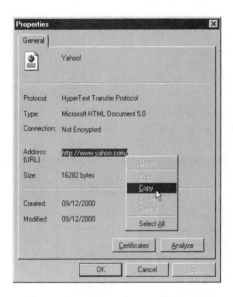

FIGURE 10.7 The Properties dialog box contains the actual URL for a framed page. You can copy the URL using the shortcut menu after you highlight the text.

Printing

Another huge problem for users of your framed Web site is *printing*. Why should printing be a problem? As much as we like to think that we are headed toward paperless offices and online commerce, people still like to print documents. When most people see a page that they want to print, they click the Print button on their browser. With older browsers, the Print button only prints the *active frame*.

Active Frame   The last frame that you clicked.

On my sample framed site, if you clicked a link in the left frame to open a new document in the main frame and then clicked the Print button without making any other mouse clicks, you would actually print the navigation bar on the left frame, not the document in the main frame that you wanted. Unfortunately, the browser doesn't know which frame you want, only which frame was last active.

The newer browser versions have included a new feature in their Print dialog boxes—a Print Frames option that allows you to specify whether you want to print the active frame or the entire frameset (see Figure 10.8). A big improvement, but you can't guarantee which browser your visitor is using.

FIGURE 10.8   The Print dialog box from Internet Explorer.

> **Tip** If you want to print a single frame, you can click the right-mouse button, or hold down the mouse button if you are using a Macintosh, and select the Print option from the shortcut menu. The printer will print only the selected frame, not the entire frameset.

Using Frames Effectively

Although frames have some usability problems, there are some obvious advantages for using them. Just make sure that you use them the right way. Here are some tips to help.

- *Frames are not a toy*   Frames work best when used as a navigation tool, or when it makes sense to show two or more elements of a document at the same time.

- *Remember the `target` attribute*   Nothing is worse than clicking a hyperlink in a framed document and breaking out of frames unintentionally. Worse, each hyperlink in a framed document that does not include the `target` attribute has the potential of opening in a new browser window. You could end up with a real mess.

- *Include the `<noframes>` tag*   Always remember that there are people who can't see frames (either because of older browsers, or because they set their browser preferences to ignore them). Provide alternate content with the `<noframes>` tag.

- *Include alternate navigation within the main frame*   With the Web, there is no guarantee that your visitors will always arrive at your home page and see the frameset as you intended them to see it. Sometimes, they will arrive on an individual frame. If you provide additional navigation links within those pages, your visitors will still be able to move within your site.

- *Never frame other framed pages*   Not as frequent anymore on the Web, but when frames first became available, Web page authors framed everything, including other framesets. This compound-framing is very confusing to users.

Table 10.1 lists the HTML tags that were discussed in this lesson.

TABLE 10.1   HTML Tags Used in This Lesson

HTML Tag	Closing	Description of Use
`<a href>`	`</a>`	Creates hyperlinks to other documents. Always use the `target` attribute with frames.
`<frameset>`	`</frameset>`	Replaces the `<body>` tag in a frameset document and surrounds the `<frame>` and `<noframes>` tags. This tag must include the attribute to describe the orientation of the frames and their size.
`<frame />`		Includes the frame's `name` and `id` and a URL for the content (`src`). It also might include attributes to define the `border` and `scrolling`.
`<iframe>`	`</iframe>`	Embeds a frame inside another document. It only works with Internet Explorer.
`<noframes>`	`</noframes>`	Defines an alternate viewing page for browsers that don't support frames.

In this lesson, you've learned:

- A frameset document defines the number of frames and their sizes; standard HTML documents will be contained in the frames.

- Each frame of a frameset document must be named so that you can direct your hyperlink to appear in a specific *target* frame.

- Despite their obvious advantage for organizing your site's navigation elements, many people dislike frames because of usability problems associated with them.

LESSON 11

Building Online Forms

In this lesson, you'll learn how to create Web forms that enable you to get input from your visitors.

Creating Forms

You've seen forms on the Web, but I'll bet you didn't know they were so easy to create. I want to point out a couple of things for you to keep track of as you read this section and then you'll create a form.

- Forms are made up of fields (that you want the user to fill out) and buttons (to perform actions such as submit and reset).

- Every field (`<input type="type" />`) should have `name` and `id` attributes as well.

- Every field can be set to have a default value (a pre-selected option that the users can overwrite if they want); many also can be set to validate the data the user enters.

- Every form requires a Submit button that sends the form data to the address specified in the `action` attribute of the `<form>` tag. It has its own `<input />` tag and you can read more about it in the "Buttons" section later in this lesson.

One more thing: A form isn't a form until it is enclosed within the `<form>` tag. The `<form>` tag always includes an `action` and a `method` attribute. To make it simple, a form's `method` is almost always set to `post` and the `action` can only be one of two values: an e-mail address of the person who will be receiving the form's data, or a URL of a file that will be receiving the form's data. We're going to use the e-mail option because it's easier for you to practice with. Figure 11.1 demonstrates an online form using the following simple `<form>` tag. Figure 11.2 shows the full HTML document for the form shown in Figure 11.1.

```
<form method="mailto:youremail@yourisp.com" action="post">
```

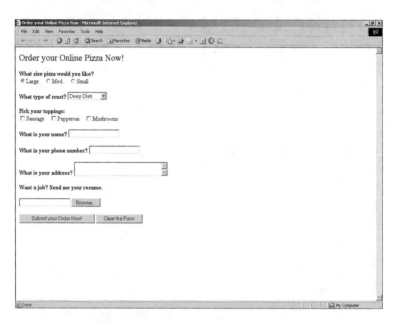

FIGURE 11.1   This Web form contains each of the input types (fields) discussed in this lesson.

Don't forget that an HTML form is just like any other HTML document; it doesn't recognize extra spaces. If you want to line up your fields for a more professional-looking form, line up your form fields in tables, as shown in Figure 11.3, and use style sheet properties to define your fonts and add images.

```
pizza_form.txt - Notepad
File  Edit  Format  Help
<!DOCTYPE html
    PUBLIC "-//W3C//DTD XHTML 1.0 Transitional//EN"
    "http://www.w3.org/TR/xhtml1/DTD/xhtml1-transitional.dtd">
<html xmlns="http://www.w3.org/1999/xhtml" xml:lang="en" lang="en">
<head>
<title>Order your Online Pizza Now</title>
</head>

<body>
<p><big><big>Order your Online Pizza Now!</big></big></p>

<form method="POST" action="mailto:pizza@pizza.com" name="pizza_order" id="pizza_order">

<p><strong>What size pizza would you like?<br></strong>
    <input type="radio" value="large" name="size" id="size" checked tabindex="1" />Large   
    <input type="radio" value="med" name="size" id="size" tabindex="2" />Med.   
    <input type="radio" value="small" name="size" id="size" tabindex="3" />Small</p>

<p><strong>What type of crust?</strong>
    <select name="crust" id="crust" size="1">
    <option value="Deep Dish" tabindex="4">Deep Dish</option>   
    <option value="Hand-Tossed" tabindex="5">Hand-Tossed</option>   
    <option value="Thin &amp; Crispy" tabindex="6">Thin &amp; Crispy</option>
    </select></p>

<p><strong>Pick your toppings:</strong><br>
    <input type="checkbox" name="toppings" id="toppings" value="sausage" tabindex="7" />Sausage   
    <input type="checkbox" name="toppings" id="toppings" value="pepperoni" tabindex="8" />Pepperoni   
    <input type="checkbox" name="toppings" id="toppings" value="mushrooms" tabindex="9" />Mushrooms</p>

    <p><strong>What is your name?</strong>
    <input type="text" name="name" id="name" size="20" tabindex="10" /></p>

<p><strong>What is your phone number?</strong>
    <input type="text" name="phone" id="phone" size="20" tabindex="11" /></p>

<p><strong>What is your address?</strong>
    <textarea rows="2" name="address" id="address" cols="30" tabindex="12">Enter the address here.</textarea></p>
<p>
<p><strong>Want a job? Send me your resume.</strong></p>
    <p><input type="file" enctype="multipart/form-data" name="resume" id="resume" tabindex="13" /></p>

<p><input type="submit" value="Submit your Order Now!" name="B1" tabindex="14" />
    <input type="reset" value="Clear the Form" name="B2" tabindex="15" /></p>
</form>
</body>
</html>
```

FIGURE 11.2 Here's the HTML document for the form shown in Figure 11.1.

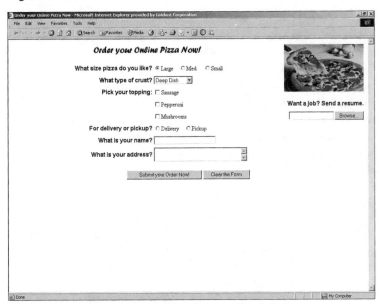

FIGURE 11.3 This version of the form took a little longer to create, but the results are worth it.

Form Fields

The main reason to create a form is to collect data. The fields on a form help you do that. The following sections describe each of the field types and give you some hints for how each one can be customized to suit your needs.

Text Box

The simplest form of data collection is an empty box. Your form poses a question ("What is your name?") and your visitor fills in the answer in the space provided. In HTML, this type of field is called a *text box*. HTML uses the <input /> command to identify a form field. The following example is a complete HTML form with one field: a text box that is 40 pixels wide and is called Name.

```
<form action="mailto:youremail@yourisp.com" method="post">
<p><b>What is your name?</b></p>
<p><input type="text" name="Name" id="Name" size="40" /></p>
<p><input type="submit" value="Submit" name="submit"
    id="submit" /></p>
</form>
```

The form field's attributes (type, name, id, and size) help to customize the form field. name, id, and size are obvious, but the type attribute could use some explanation. Although this type of field traditionally is called a *text* box, you also can set the type attribute to password (which displays an asterisk when the user types his or her password). If you know that your visitors will be using Internet Explorer, you could also set the type attribute to integer (which is a whole number without decimals) or number (which can include decimals). One more type, file, is explained in the "File Select" section found later.

 Tip The tabindex attribute, shown within the <input /> tags on Figure 11.2, sets the order in which the user can navigate through the form elements using the Tab key. The tabindex attribute and the index number increases toward the bottom of the form.

Text Area

You use the `<textarea>` tag to define a multiline text box. In addition to the usual `name`, `id`, and `tabindex` attributes, all `<textarea>` boxes should control the size of the box using the `rows` and `cols` attributes. `cols` indicates the width of the field in pixels; `rows` indicates the height of the field.

Anything you type between the `<textarea>` and `</textarea>` tags will appear inside the field and can be overwritten by users when they are completing the form. The following example shows the code for a text area box with an initial value of "Enter the address here."

```
<textarea rows="2" name="address" id="address"
cols="30" tabindex="12">Enter the address here.</textarea>
```

Radio Buttons and Check Boxes

Radio button and check box fields are very similar. In fact, there's really only one difference between them: Your user can select only one item in a radio button list, but can select multiple check box items. Look at the form in Figure 11.1 again. Check boxes are used for the pizza toppings question because it is possible that your visitors might want multiple toppings. Radio buttons are used to ask about the preferred size of the pizza because a pizza can only be one size.

The following example demonstrates how a check box field is created. Notice all the check box fields that relate to the same question ("Pick your toppings") have the same `name` and `id` attributes. You use the `value` attribute to specify the information you will see when the form data is submitted to you. If you don't specify any `value`, the form data typically will send `on/off` or `yes/no` values for all fields.

```
<p><strong>Pick your toppings:</strong><br>
<input type="checkbox" name="toppings" id="toppings"
  value="sausage" tabindex="7" />
    Sausage   
<input type="checkbox" name="toppings" id="toppings"
  value="pepperoni" tabindex="8" />
    Pepperoni   
<input type="checkbox" name="toppings" id="toppings"
  value="mushrooms" tabindex="9" />
    Mushrooms</p>
```

With radio buttons, you'll need to use the checked attribute to set a starting value for each field. When you do specify a preselected option, be sure to select the most frequently submitted value. In the following example, the large pizza has been preselected. Users can change that selection when they are completing the form and the form data will be submitted to you with the users' choices selected.

```
<p><strong>What size pizza would you like?<br></strong>
    <input type="radio" value="large" name="size"
     id="size" checked tabindex="1" />
        Large   
    <input type="radio" value="med" name="size"
     id="size" tabindex="2" />
        Med.   
    <input type="radio" value="small" name="size"
     id="size" tabindex="3" />
        Small</p>
```

Drop-Down Option

The drop-down menu option, shown in the following HTML sample, uses a <select> tag to define the overall menu (such as giving it a name, id, and a size—the number of rows visible at any time). Enclosed within the <select> tag are <option> tags that describe the contents of the drop-down menu. As with radio buttons, you can specify a start value for the drop-down menu using the selected attribute.

```
<p><strong>What type of crust?</strong>
    <select name="crust" id="crust" size="1">
        <option value="Deep Dish" tabindex="4">
            Deep Dish</option>   
        <option value="Hand-Tossed" tabindex="5">
            Hand-Tossed</option>   
        <option value="Thin &amp; Crispy" tabindex="6">
            Thin &amp; Crispy</option>
    </select></p>
```

Drop-Down Default

Some form designers like to add an <option> tag at the top of their drop-down menu fields that tells their users to select one of the items from the list. The following code sample demonstrates how this option would look. Figure 11.4 illustrates this option in an online form.

```
<option value="Pick">Pick One</option>
```

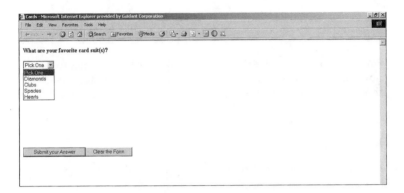

FIGURE 11.4 This drop-down menu includes an extra <option> tag for the Pick One statement.

Like check boxes, your user can hold the Ctrl key to select multiple options in the drop-down menu if you add the `multiple` attribute to the `<select>` tag. This change (shown in the following HTML sample) enables users to select multiple options by pressing and holding down the Ctrl key while clicking on the options in the menu. (See Figure 11.5.)

```
<form action="mailto:youremail@yourisp.com" method="post">
<h3>What are your favorite card suit(s)?</h3>
<select name="suit" id="suit" size="1" multiple="multiple">
    <option value="Hearts">Hearts</option>
    <option value="Diamonds">Diamonds</option>
    <option value="Clubs">Clubs</option>
    <option value="Spades">Spades</option>
</select>
<p><input type="submit" value="Submit your Answer"
name="submit" id="submit" />
<input type="reset" value="Clear the Form" name="reset"
id="reset" /></p>
</form>
```

FIGURE 11.5 Changing the `size="1"` attribute from the drop-down menu code sample to `size="3"` enables the visitor to see three options at once. Here, two options have been selected.

File Select

Another useful way to gather information from your visitors is to allow them to send you files. You might use this input option, the `file` type, to collect résumés, orders, or any other type of file. The following HTML sample demonstrates how this option is created. As you can see in Figure 11.6, the browser creates a Browse button to help your visitors send their files.

```
<form action="mailto:youremail@yourisp.com" method="post">
<p>Send me your resume.</p>
<p><input type="file" enctype="multipart/form-data"
          name="resume" id="resume" /></p>
<p><input type="submit" value="send now"
          name="submit" id="submit" /></p>
</form>
```

Send me your resume.

[   ] Browse...

send now

FIGURE 11.6 The visitors will click the Browse button to browse their own file system in search of the appropriate file.

Caution Check with your Web host before creating this type of form; it might have additional requirements for you.

Buttons

The Submit and Reset buttons are special types of form elements. Although they are created using the `<input />` tag (see Figure 11.2), they are not data collection tools, but actually are data submission tools.

- The Submit button collects all the data from the form and *posts* (sends) it to the location specified in the `action` portion of the `<form>` tag.

- The Reset button clears the form of any data that might have already been completed. The Reset button *resets* the form to the original pre-selected values.

The Submit button is required on all forms, but the Reset button is optional. The browser's Refresh button has the same effect as the Reset button on a form. It reloads the page and deletes everything except the initial values of the form.

Tip There is one more input type to be aware of: the hidden type. A hidden field is not displayed on the form, but returns results anyway. You might want to collect the date and time the visitor submitted the form, the version of the form that was submitted, or the name of the person who should receive the data. Create the field based on the HTML example that follows:

```
<input type="hidden" name="version"
       id="version" value="B" />
```

Receiving Form Data

When your visitors click the Submit button on a form on your Web site, the data they entered into the form will be sent to you using the `action` you specified in your `<form>` tag. In Figure 11.2, we selected an e-mail `action`. Figure 11.7 shows you how my e-mail software returns the form data to me. You should now see why it is so important to include the `name` and `id` attributes associated with every form field.

FIGURE 11.7   Your e-mail software may format the responses differently, but they will all show the field names (Size and Toppings, for example), along with the data your visitor entered into those fields.

It is not always convenient to receive form data via e-mail, particularly if you expect to receive a lot of responses. Reading, and responding to, that many e-mail messages can become tiresome. Your ISP also might prefer that you do not use its mail servers in this manner.

Another `action` that you can assign to your forms is a script to handle the responses for you. Scripts are automated form handlers and can be used to collect all the responses in a single file and respond to the visitors for you. This book can't begin to explain how to write the scripts, or find them, but your ISP, or your network administrator, probably will have several scripts available for you to choose from and can help you attach them to your form.

Caution   All ISPs handle forms differently. Always check with your ISP or network administrator before attempting to create forms for your Web site.

Table 11.1 lists the HTML tags that were discussed in this lesson.

TABLE 11.1   HTML Tags Used in This Lesson

HTML Tag	Closing	Description of Use
`<form>`	`</form>`	Encloses all form elements.
`<input />`		Identifies a form field.
`<option>`	`</option>`	Identifies the contents of a drop menu.
`<select>`	`</select>`	Encloses a drop-down menu field.
`<textarea>`	`</textarea>`	Identifies a multi-lined text field.

In this lesson, you've learned:

- All form fields should have name, id, and tabindex attributes.

- The `<form>` tag always includes a method attribute (which is usually post) and an action attribute. The action can be either an e-mail address or a URL of a file that will be receiving the form's data.

- The six form field types are text box, text area, radio buttons, check boxes, drop-down option menus, and the file browse box.

LESSON 12
Making It Sing: Sound and Video

In this lesson, you'll learn how to add sound and video to your Web pages, and find the plug-ins required to use them.

Adding Sound and Video

Used correctly, sound and video clips can greatly enhance the content in your Web pages. Imagine a Web page about Dr. Martin Luther King, Jr. that didn't include something about his famous "I Have a Dream" speech. The text of the speech is moving, but the delivery is what made it so powerful. You can add sound and video clips to your own Web pages using some HTML tags you've already learned.

> **Tip**   You can hear the "I Have a Dream" speech at `http://www.americanrhetoric.com/speeches/Ihaveadream.htm`.

This lesson discusses several methods for adding sound and video clips. You should know that the one method that is sure to work with every browser on every platform is also the simplest: the <a> tag.

```
<a href="http://www.americanrhetoric.com/mp3clips/
politicalspeeches/mlkihaveadream35348.mp3">
Listen to the I Have a Dream speech.</a>
```

When your visitors click on the words *Listen to the I Have a Dream speech*, the `mlkihaveadream35348.mp3` file will download to their computers and begin playing. If the visitors do not have the correct plug-in to hear the sound clip, the browser should prompt them to save the file for later. It will not, however, prompt them to download the correct plug-in. You will need to provide that information on your page.

Tip Try typing "sound clips" into your favorite search engine to find sound files you could use on your own pages.

Video clips can be handled in exactly the same way:

```
<a href="
    http://www.lucidcafe.com/library/96jan/96jangifs/
    MLK630828Video.ram">
Watch a video of Dr. King's greatest speech.</a>
```

Caution Use sound and video sparingly and make the wait worthwhile. Even short clips can have a large file size and may take a very long time to load. Make sure that you give your visitors some idea of the content of the clip so that they can decide whether to wait for the download.

\<embed\>

Netscape invented a new tag called \<embed\> to enable you to include a sound or video clip on a Web page. Microsoft's Internet Explorer browser also accepts this non-standard tag. The following sample shows how the \<embed\> tag works to add a video clip.

Tip If you'd like to duplicate the following sample, you can download the video clip from http:// download.microsoft.com/download/0/9/d/09d051c4- decc-4d39-9c57-f520187213a1/Amazing_Caves_720.exe and save it to your own desktop. Then just change the src attribute to suit your needs.

```
<p>Click the video to see a clip from the IMAX movie Journey
   into Amazing Caves.</p>
     <embed src="C:\Documents and
       Settings\qc04818\Desktop\Amazing_Caves_720.wmv"
       width="360" controls="true" autostart="true"
       loop="false">
         <noembed>
           <a href="C:\Documents and
             Settings\qc04818\Desktop\Amazing_Caves_720.wmv">
             Click for a surprise.</a>
         </noembed>
     </embed>
<p>You will need the <a href="http://www.microsoft.com/
     windows/windowsmedia/download/
     AllDownloads.aspx?displang=en&qstechnology=">
     Windows Media Player</a> to see this clip.</p>
```

The browser displays the control panel for the media device you use, as
shown in Figure 12.1. You can add width and height attributes to the
<embed> tag to control the size of the video still. The <noembed> tag
provides an alternate way for visitors to download the video if their
browser doesn't recognize the <embed> tag.

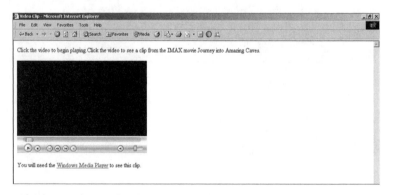

FIGURE 12.1   When embedded, a control panel for the device
used to play the video or sound clip, appears in the browser.

Notice that I've included four attributes for the <embed> tag in this
example: width, controls, autostart and loop. Width sets the width of
the video. It is not necessary to set the height since the video will size the
image proportionally. Controls ensures that the video player controls are

included. Autostart, which you can set to true or false, tells the browser whether to begin playing the clip immediately upon loading the page. The loop attribute tells the browser how many times in a row to play the clip before stopping. You can set the loop attribute to any whole number.

Another attribute you can set is autorewind. This attribute is automatically set to true, but if for some reason you *don't* want to rewind the clip after it plays, you can set it to false. The hidden attribute hides the player's VCR controls from the user. Hiding the controls gives you, the developer, more control over the use of the clip, but may annoy your visitors if they are not allowed to turn your clip on or off.

<object>

The <embed> tag is nonstandard, which means that the W3C doesn't recognize it as a legitimate HTML markup tag. The W3C prefers that Web page developers include sound and video clips using the <object> tag. You will learn more about this tag in Lesson 14, "Creating Active Web Pages."

```
<p>Click the video to begin playing.</p>
    <object classid="C:\Documents and
    Settings\qc04818\Desktop\Amazing_Caves_720.wmv">
    </object>
<a href="C:\Documents and
    Settings\qc04818\Desktop\Amazing_Caves_720.wmv">Surprise!</a>
```

 Caution Unfortunately, the <object> tag does not yet work consistently in all browsers, although it is the W3C-preferred tagging method. Be prepared to either always include an alternate <a href> tag for sound and video elements, or duplicate your work by including the <embed> tag as well.

The <object> tag also comes with a multitude of attributes that you can set to help control the use of the clip in your Web page. You can add a border around the object by using the appearance attribute and setting the value to 1. The <object> tag also has an autostart and autorewind attribute.

Finding Plug-ins

We've mentioned before that it's never a good idea to include any items on your Web page that require a plug-in (such as Flash or RealAudio) without also providing a link to the plug-in. You don't want to assume that your visitors will have the required software to view your page because they might not.

Microsoft generally believes that the browser itself should contain enough code to run any scripts, applications, and embedded items without loading plug-ins, and it uses ActiveX controls to handle these types of events. Netscape, however, agrees with the idea that browsers should be light and plug-ins should be used to handle outside events. Partially because of this belief, Netscape maintains one of the best plug-in archives on the Web at `http://browser.netscape.com/ns8/community/plugin.jsp`.

 Tip   If you're looking for a browser-neutral source of downloadable plug-ins, check out CNET at `http://www.download.com/sort/3120-20-0-1-5.html?qt=browser+plug-ins`.

Table 12.1 lists the HTML tags that were discussed in this lesson.

TABLE 12.1   HTML Tags Used in This Lesson

HTML Tag	Closing	Description of Use
`<embed>`	`</embed>`	Netscape's nonstandard, although largely supported, tag for including sound and video clips.
`<noembed>`	`</noembed>`	Netscape's tag that provides an alternate method of downloading the clip for browsers that don't recognize the `<embed>` tag.
`<object>`	`</object>`	W3C's preferred, although largely unsupported, tag for including sound and video clips.

In this lesson, you've learned:

- Sound and video clips can be added to your Web page with the `<a>` tag.

- Both the `<object>` and the `<embed>` tags enable you to add a video clip with the video controls (start, stop, and so on) to your documents.

LESSON 13
Designing with HTML

In this lesson, you will learn some designer tricks of the trade to make your pages look as good as they work.

Design Basics

Web design may have had its roots in traditional paper design, but online design is different. One of the biggest differences when designing for online is the capability to *hyperlink*. Adding hyperlinks in your Web pages gives you the capability to quickly direct your viewers to the information you want them to see, including reference material on, or off, your Web site. Unfortunately, the capability to link also is one of the biggest disadvantages to online design. Occasionally, viewers get so caught up in clicking on all those "for additional information click here" links that they forget what they were looking for in the first place; in effect, they get lost in cyberspace.

Web site designers have a number of design elements available to help them make it easy for their users to recognize which Web pages are part of the same Web site. These elements can also help set the mood for their Web site. The layout, images, navigation buttons, bullets, lines, colors, and even the fonts you choose should support the overall design theme of your site. In the following sections, you'll learn how each of these elements works together.

To design an effective Web page, you'll need to be aware of the differences in moving from traditional design to online design. Table 13.1 summarizes some of the differences. Knowing the problems you'll face is only half the battle; the rest is knowing how to avoid them. You'll learn that in the sections that follow.

TABLE 13.1   Paper Design Versus Online Design

Paper Design	Online Design
Viewers follow content along a linear path with a beginning, middle, and an end.	Using search tools or hyperlinks, viewers can access the content at any point. The only way for you to control that movement is to provide hyperlinks and navigation.
Viewers can see an entire page (text and graphics) at the same time.	With larger graphics (or non-graphical browsers), viewers often have time to read the entire text before they ever see any images.
Serif fonts (such as Times Roman) usually are used for content; sans-serif fonts (such as Arial) usually are used for headings.	Sans-serif fonts usually are used for content; serif fonts usually are used for headings.
Viewers see an entire page (or multiple pages in a book or magazine layout). The size of the page, and the amount of content presented on it, are controlled by you, the author.	Viewers see only the amount of content that will fit on their monitor at one time, which often is only a couple of paragraphs of text. The viewer controls the presentation of the content with the size of their monitor and the browser settings.

Two whole fields of study, Information Design and Usability, are devoted to finding the most effective methods of communicating your message. Researchers in these fields have come up with some standard design guidelines that can help you make the most of the material you have to present. Following are some facts I'll bet you didn't know:

- Red, yellow, orange, and green are the most difficult colors of text to read online. It's best not to use them or to use them sparingly. You'll learn more about colors and fonts in the subsequent sections.

- Your visitors read almost 50% slower online than on paper. You can counter that by keeping your page length short (no more than two to three screen lengths) and providing tables and bulleted lists to give their eyes a rest from large blocks of text.

- Animated images and moving text catch the eye of potential visitors, but most people find them annoying if they continue to move while the visitor is trying to read or search for content on the page. You'll learn about these features in Lesson 14, "Creating Active Web Pages."

- If your visitors are looking for a particular piece of information, they will search your site for less than a minute before moving on to some other site, unless they are confident that you have the information they are looking for. A well-designed Web site will help your visitors find their information quickly. You'll learn how to do this in the "Layout, Content, and Navigation" section.

Layout, Content, and Navigation

Because people tend to read online text more slowly than paper text, Web site designers use *page layout* techniques to help make content more readable.

Page Layout   The arrangement of text, graphics, and *whitespace* on a page.

Whitespace   Refers to the background of a page. Note that this space does not have to be white.

In general, when designing a Web site, you will need to keep the following key tips in mind. Figure 13.1 shows you how some of these layout tricks work to emphasize your content.

- *Keep paragraphs short and include a margin*   Keep your paragraphs under ten lines and include a margin. If you want viewers to read your text, you'll need to make it easy for them. You learned how to use style sheets to create margins in Lesson 5, "Adding Your Own Style."

* *Break up long sections of text with bullets, tables, and headings* Information design research has shown that online readers scan text, rather than read it, until they find what they're looking for. Bullets and headings help users find things more quickly.

* *Don't underline any text unless it is a hyperlink* Online viewers expect anything underlined to be clickable. If you use underlining for another purpose, such as formatting your headings, you will confuse your readers.

A plain text document can be boring and intimidating.

Headings break up the text, but it's still boring.

Adding bullets and a paragraph separator helps add diversity and interest to your page.

FIGURE 13.1 Adding diversity to your page layout helps enhance its readability.

If your Web site contains more than one page, you'll want to include some way for your visitors to find the other pages in your site. A good navigation system is more than a table of contents; it is a defined structure that gives your visitors information about your site. Your navigation system can consist of text links or image links (refer to Lesson 8, "Using Graphics"). Whichever link type you choose, your navigation system should appear on every page of your site to help orient your users.

Tip Many designers use *frames* as a navigation tool. A frame is a portion of your HTML document that displays a separate HTML. You learned how to create frames, and use them effectively, in Lesson 10, "Creating Frames."

Fonts and Colors

Color is an exciting way to add interest to your Web pages. In addition to the obvious splash of color that images provide, you can add color to your fonts and page backgrounds. Be creative in your choices, but use a critical eye to review the results. Some colors are very difficult to read online and some color combinations are nearly impossible to decipher. Always provide some contrast in your color choice: use a light-colored font on a dark background and a dark-colored font on a light background.

Tip In HTML, some colors are defined by name (such as navy, red, and black), others by a hexadecimal number. The six-digit number represents the amount of RGB (red, green, and blue) in the color. Lynda Weinmann, a well known graphic designer, has created a couple of color charts specifically for online use: http://www.lynda.com/hex.html.

So, how do you add color? With style sheet properties, of course. HTML does have a <font> tag that enables you to specify a font (such as Arial or Times Roman) and colors and sizes, but according to the W3C, users are not supposed to use it. Instead, they've given you the font-family, font-size, color, and background properties for your style sheets. The following code provides an example of how you can specify your fonts for the <body> and <h1> tags.

Caution Just because you can specify a font doesn't mean that your visitor will have that font on his or her computer. To be on the safe side, always specify at least one alternate font, as I did in the following example. All but the most basic computers will have Arial and Times New Roman, so it's not a bad idea to use one of those two as your alternate font. Appendix B, "Style Sheet Quick Reference," contains a list of Web-safe fonts.

```
<!DOCTYPE html
     PUBLIC "-//W3C//DTD XHTML 1.0 Transitional//EN"
     "http://www.w3.org/TR/xhtml1/DTD/xhtml1-
transitional.dtd">
<html xmlns="http://www.w3.org/1999/xhtml"
      xml:lang="en" lang="en">
<head>
<title>Fonts and Colors</title>
<style type="text/css">
body {font-family:Trebuchet MS, Arial;
      color:navy;
      font-size:12;
      background:white}
h1    {font-family:Bookman Old Style, Times New Roman;
      color:white;
      font-size:14;
      background:navy}
</style>
</head>
<body>
<h1>Fonts and Colors</h1>
<p>This text is navy on a white background, but the heading
   above is white on a navy background.</p>
</body>
</html>
```

By changing the values in the style properties, you change the results you see in the browser. Look at Figure 13.2 to see how the following changes affect what you see. By not adding a separate font-color and background property to the <h1> tag, the properties assigned in the <body> tag continue.

```
<style type="text/css">
body {font-family:Trebuchet MS;
      color:black;
      font-size:12;
      background:#FFFF80}
h1   {font-family:Bookman Old Style;
      font-size:14}
</style>
```

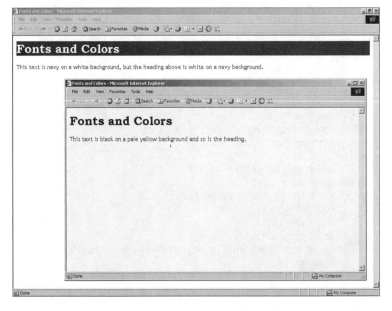

FIGURE 13.2   The background property sets the background color of the entire tag, so using the property on the <body> tag sets the color for the entire page.

Tip   Don't get carried away with your font selections. A good rule of thumb is to use no more than three different fonts on each page: one font for the headings, one for the body text, and one for any special text, such as captions and pull-quotes.

Images

Like the other design elements discussed in this lesson, you should use images sparingly when they support the theme you've already established. In Lesson 8, you learned how to add images to your Web pages and use HTML and style sheet properties to align them with your text. Figure 13.3 shows the difference that balance and diversity make to your overall Web page layout.

Alternating the placement of
the images helps balance the
page, but it's still boring.

Placing all the images
on one side of the page
makes it seem off
balance and boring.

Balancing the images
with text and whitespace
makes the most
creative use of your page.

FIGURE 13.3 Adding diversity to your graphical layout helps add interest.

Caution Whenever you are working with graphics on a Web page, you need to be mindful of the overall size of the page. Most people will visit your Web site using a slow modem connection and might not be willing to wait for your page to finish loading. When you open your page using a modem, it should take no longer than five seconds to load. If your pages take much longer to load, you might try to reduce the image size, add thumbnails, or include some type of warning as to the fact that the page will take longer to load.

Background Images

Earlier, you learned how to add background color to your pages, but sometimes you'll want to add an image to the background of your page. The most prolific example of a background image is the page border (see Figure 13.4).

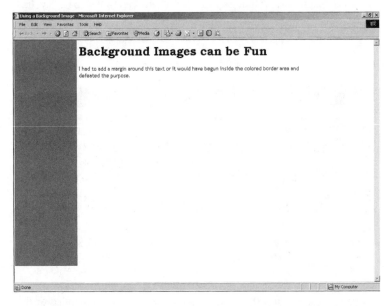

FIGURE 13.4   Use the background-image and margin style sheet properties to create a colored border on your Web page.

Here's how the source code looks for that page:

```
<!DOCTYPE html
      PUBLIC "-//W3C//DTD XHTML 1.0 Transitional//EN"
      "http://www.w3.org/TR/xhtml1/DTD/xhtml1-
transitional.dtd">
<html xmlns="http://www.w3.org/1999/xhtml"
      xml:lang="en" lang="en">
<head>
<title>Using a Background Image</title>
<style type="text/css">
body {font-family:Trebuchet MS, Arial;
      color:black;
```

```
        font-size:14;
        background-image:url(images\background.gif);
        background-repeat:no repeat);
        background-position:left top;
        margin:10px,160px}
h1      {font-family:Bookman Old Style, Times New Roman;
        color:#A00068;
        font-size:18;
        background:white}
</style>
</head>
<body>
<h1>Background Images can be Fun</h1>
<p>I had to add a margin around this text or it would have
    begun inside the colored border area and defeated
    the purpose.</p>
</body>
</html>
```

The background.gif image is the colored border background. It is a GIF file, which makes it small (only 5KB) so that it will load quickly. I made it in Paint Shop Pro by drawing a rectangle down the side of the page, as shown in Figure 13.5.

FIGURE 13.5   The background.gif file was created in Paint Shop Pro.

You've already seen how you can use style sheet properties to set the fonts and colors of the page, but look at the previous HTML source code for Figure 13.4 again to see that we've added four new style sheet properties for you to learn:

- `Background-image:url` *(URL of file)*   The property tells the browser where to find the background image you want to use on your page. It must be used as part of the body style.

- `Background-position`   This property tells the browser where to place the background image. This is assumed to be the top left (or left top), but you can specify any combination of the following vertical values: `top`, `bottom`, or `center`, and these horizontal values: `left`, `right`, or `center`.

- `Background-repeat`   This property determines whether or not the background image will repeat in a tiled manner to file the entire browser window or appear on the background just once.

- `Margin`   You can specify the margin property in inches (`in`), centimeters (`cm`), ems (`em`), points (`pt`), or pixels (`px`). If no unit of measure is specified, the pixel unit is assumed. You can set the top, right, bottom, and left margins. I only set two of the margins for my background (0, 160). The browser knows that I wanted `top=0px`, `right=160px`, `bottom=0px`, and `left=160px`. The browser copied the first two values and applied the same values to the last two options. If I had entered only one value, the browser would have applied the same value to all four options.

If I hadn't set the `margin` property, the text on my page would have overlapped my image, as shown in Figure 13.6.

 Tip   Don't forget to check out Lesson 5 if you want to know more about HTML style sheets.

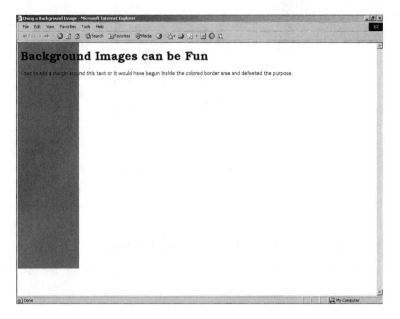

FIGURE 13.6   Without the margin property, text starts at the left edge of the page.

In this lesson, you've learned:

- The layout, images, navigation buttons, bullets, lines, colors, and even the fonts that you choose should support the overall design theme of your site.

- Create interest in your Web pages by alternating the alignment of text and images, and by adding bulleted lists and tables.

- Just because you can specify a font doesn't mean that your visitor will have that font on his or her computer. To be on the safe side, always use Arial or Times New Roman as your alternate font.

LESSON 14
Creating Active Web Pages

In this lesson, you will learn about some of the advanced scripting tools that can enhance your Web pages. You'll also find some resources to help you learn more.

What Are Active Web Pages?

Normal HTML pages—everything you've created so far—are considered to be *static*. The page you create is the page that your visitors see, and (assuming that the pages are created without browser-specific code) all your visitors see the same thing.

Scripting languages and DHTML provide the capability to make any HTML element respond to user events, such as mouse clicks. This capability can be used for something as simple as displaying a menu of navigational choices when a word is clicked, to something as complex as a Web application, like online ordering.

Don't be scared off by the word *application*. There is some programming knowledge that is required to implement these elements into your Web pages, but not much. Unfortunately, I can't teach you everything there is to know about programming, but I can tell you where to find additional information.

The most popular ways of including active elements in your Web pages are described in the sections that follow. Table 14.1 gives a quick overview of the information in this lesson.

TABLE 14.1 Scripting and Programming

Technique	Comments
ActiveX	ActiveX works natively on Microsoft Internet Explorer and on Netscape with a plug-in.

Technique	Comments
DHTML	Microsoft and Netscape disagree on how to implement DHTML. You might end up creating two sets of code to make everyone happy.
Java	Platform independent and can be used to create complex applications.
JavaScript	The best of everything. Works on all the major browsers, can be called from a plain HTML page, and you can find plenty of examples to copy into your own Web pages.
VBScript	An easy to learn scripting language, VBScript is the most commonly used language in creating Active Server Pages.

DHTML

DHTML is an acronym for *Dynamic HTML*. DHTML combines all the elements you've already learned (HTML, style sheets, and scripting) to create Web pages that are interactive and easy to update. Unfortunately, Microsoft, Netscape, and the World Wide Web Consortium (W3C) all disagree on how to accomplish this feat. The W3C doesn't even list the acronym on its Web site when discussing HTML standards.

 Tip See what Microsoft has to say about DHTML at `http://msdn.microsoft.com/library/default.asp?url=/workshop/author/dhtml/dhtml.asp`.

You can find Netscape's description at `http://archive.devx.com/dhtml/articles/sl011701/sl011701.asp`.

Microsoft and Netscape do agree that DHTML should enable you to alter the appearance of a Web page after it has been loaded in the browser. They also agree that DHTML should enable developers to position any HTML element on a page. The elements can even be positioned in the same location so that, in effect, the elements appear on top of each other, but that's where the agreement ends.

Microsoft and Netscape have each developed their own browser-specific codes to achieve this type of interactivity. Using Microsoft's coding standards means that Netscape viewers might not be able to see the dynamic elements. The same is true if you use Netscape's coding standards. This diversity means that developers are forced to choose either to ignore a whole subset of their users, or to double-code all their pages to ensure that doesn't happen.

The most popular use of DHTML on the Internet is in navigational menus. You've seen it in action even if you didn't recognize it. When you hover over a menu name and a list of submenus appears, the menu was probably generated using DHTML. One of my favorite examples (shown in Figure 14.1) includes images as well as text links in the submenus.

 Tip   You can find plenty of information and coding examples online at http://www.DynamicDrive.com.

Figure 14.1   This Web site uses style sheets, absolute positioning, and JavaScript to dynamically alter the page.

Java and ActiveX

Java and ActiveX are both programming languages used to create Web applications. Java (created by Sun Microsystems) is platform independent (meaning that PCs, Macs, and UNIX systems can interpret the commands in the application). ActiveX (created by Microsoft), however, only works with the Internet Explorer browser. It is nearly impossible to guarantee that your visitors will use this browser unless you employ the annoying tactic that so many developers have chosen: preceding any application with a note warning your visitors that they must download the *correct* browser before they can view your pages.

How Do They Work?

Both Java and ActiveX work under the principle of object-oriented programming. The idea is that each piece of code should be treated as a separate entity, which can be used repeatedly in many types of environments, including the Web.

Both elements can be embedded in your Web pages using HTML's `<object>` tag. An `<object>`, in HTML, can be an image, an application, or another HTML document. The attributes are the important distinction. The first example (which follows) would be used to include a Java applet. The second example would be used to include an ActiveX control (or application).

```
<object codetype="application/java-archive"
        codebase="http://www.myWeb.com/apps/"
        classid="java:my.program.start">
</object>

<object codebase="http://www.myWeb.com/apps/"
        data="my.activex.program">
        classid="CLSID:613C8CCE-1FF8-41CF-A3DB-052336C14002"
</object>
```

In the first example, the `classid` attribute is the name of the Java applet being called by the `<object>` tag. This same information appears in the `data` attribute for ActiveX programs. In both examples, the `codebase` attribute indicates the directory in which the application can be found. However, the `codebase` attribute itself is not necessary. The entire URL (including the base directory information) could be included in the classid (for Java) and data (for ActiveX) attributes rather than including the separate codebase attribute.

The ActiveX classid attribute deserves some explanation. Other than telling you that the string of letters and numbers actually represents a URL, the best help I can give is to inform you that any ActiveX control that you choose to use in your Web page includes the appropriate classid information so that you can copy it into your tag.

Tip   Find information about Java and download some fun Java applets at
`http://java.sun.com/applets/index.html.`

You can download ActiveX controls at
`http://www.download.com/2001-2206-0.html.`

JavaScript and VBScript

Scripting is another type of programming, but it's easier to learn, which is a plus. Scripts can be added to an HTML document using the <script> tag. The tag can appear within the <head> or <body> of the document.

A script might be contained in a separate document that is called by the <script> tag (much as a linked style sheet is a separate document called by the <style> tag). A script might also be contained within the <script> tags in the HTML document itself. The decision is yours, based on how often you plan to use the script. If the script appears in only one page, incorporate the script into the document, as in the first of the following HTML samples. If the script appears on more than one page, make it a separate file so that you don't have to duplicate it, as in the second HTML sample.

```
<script type="text/vbscript">enter your script here.</script>
<script type="text/javascript"
        src="http://www.myweb.com/scripts/myscript.jss">
</script>
```

Although the src (source) attribute is only required when the script is contained in a separate file, the type attribute is always required. This attribute tells the browser which language the script is written in: text/javascript, text/vbscript, or text/tcl. If you are using the same scripting language throughout your HTML document, you can include a <meta> tag that defines the default script type for the entire document. The <meta> tag (as you learned in Lesson 3, "Adding Text and More") is placed inside the <head> tag and gives the browser information about the document.

```
<meta http-equiv="Content-Script-Type" content="type">
```

What Can Scripting Do?

The easy answer to this question is anything. If you look at some of the script collections on the Web, you find that people are using script for all kinds of things—including adding table values, creating rollover effects, and even games.

 Tip   WebDeveloper has more than 7,000 download-able JavaScript samples at http://webdeveloper.com/ javascript/.

It is possible to associate a script with a certain event that occurs when the page appears on the browser. Figure 14.2 is an HTML page with some very simple JavaScript code that changes the background color of the page with the press of a button.

You might wonder where the code is because the <script> tag is empty. The code, in this case, is embedded in the <input> tag with the onclick command. The tag responds to each of the events shown in Table 14.2 and a few more.

FIGURE 14.2 Simple JavaScript code to change the background color with the onclick command.

TABLE 14.2 Script Calls

Event	With Tags	The Script Runs When...
onload	<body>, <frameset>	The document opens.
onunload	<body>, <frameset>	The document closes.
onclick	Anything	The mouse is clicked over a particular item (button, image, and so on).
ondblclick	Anything	The mouse is double-clicked over a particular item.
onmouseover	Anything	The mouse is moved onto an item.
onmouseout	Anything	The mouse moves away from an item.
onmousemove	Anything	The mouse is moved while on an item.
onsubmit	Submit button	The form is submitted.
onreset	Reset button	The form is reset.

Tip   The event handlers (script calls) that tags support differ between browsers. Netscape supports many fewer event handlers than Internet Explorer does. Use Web Developer Journal's compatibility table (`http://webdevelopersjournal.com/articles/ javascript_limitations.html`) to choose the right handler for your pages.

The scope of this book does not allow for coverage of all these topics in any depth, but I hope you have some idea of the possibilities and can take the time to learn more on your own. Table 14.3 lists the HTML tags that were discussed in this lesson.

TABLE 14.3   HTML Tags Used in This Lesson

HTML Tag	Closing	Description of Use
`<object>`	`</object>`	Embeds an object, such as an application, into a Web page.
`<script>`	`</script>`	Embeds a script into a Web page.

In this lesson, you've learned:

- How to add Java and ActiveX applications to your HTML documents with the `<object>` tag.

- How to add JavaScript and VBScript to your HTML documents with the `<script>` tag.

- That DHTML combines all HTML, style sheets, and scripting to create Web pages that are interactive and easy to update.

LESSON 15

Using Web Authoring Tools

In this lesson, you will learn where to find some of the most popular Web page authoring tools and how you can use them to create your Web site.

Why Use a Tool?

You've just spent the last 14 lessons learning how to create Web pages by yourself, so why would you want to use a tool? The biggest reasons are time and ease of use. The Web is a very visual medium and staring at HTML code in a text editor is not very visually stimulating. It's easy to forget to be creative when you are concentrating so hard on making sure that you're using the correct HTML tags and putting them in the proper place in the document.

Web page authoring tools come with enough bells and whistles to get your Web site started in no time, and feature excellent site management and reporting tools. There are differences, though. FrontPage, for example, comes with a set of design themes that you can apply to your own pages to give your site a professional look. Dreamweaver has extensive support for style sheets. You can easily create style sheet declarations and apply them to the other pages in your Web site.

FrontPage and Dreamweaver are consistently voted best of the best and you might find that one of them could help you, too. In the following sections, I want to introduce you to some of the most interesting features of both products.

Microsoft FrontPage

FrontPage contains a little bit of everything. It has site management features, pre-designed Web themes, starter Webs that are ready for your content, and advanced features (such as navigation buttons and search bots); all with a familiar interface that feels like a combination of Microsoft Word and the Windows Explorer. Figure 15.1 shows a sample page in FrontPage.

FIGURE 15.1 A sample page in FrontPage.

One of the best features FrontPage has going for it, aside from the fact that the interface is so familiar to most computer users, is that it includes a variety of Web wizards that you can use to define the type of site and the type of pages you want to have. Select a design theme and the program creates all your pages and adds Navigation bars with the hyperlinks already in place. You just add the basic content in the middle of the page.

The Navigation view of FrontPage is exciting as well. You can add, remove, and rearrange the pages in your Web site and FrontPage automatically updates the Navigation bar. (See Figure 15.2.)

FIGURE 15.2   The Navigation view in FrontPage. You can add, remove, and rearrange pages in this view and the Navigation bar is automatically updated.

FrontPage is available with the Professional Special Edition version of Office; it can also be purchased separately. It integrates well with the other Microsoft Office software packages, such as Word, Excel, and Access. You can even create a Web page in Microsoft Word, save it as a Web page in your FrontPage Web site, and apply the FrontPage Web theme to the finished product without losing your original formatting.

FrontPage supports basic database interactivity well. It can create and update an Access database from a form. In addition, extensive toolbars, menu choices, and shortcut menus make it easy to add your content without cluttering up the editing window. The tabs at the bottom of the

FrontPage window enable you to see the actual HTML source code for your page or a split version of the screen so that you can see both the design and code view. (See Figure 15.3.)

FIGURE 15.3 The Split view of FrontPage.

FrontPage has another feature that you might enjoy using on your Web sites. It includes the capability to add content from some of Microsoft's most popular Web sites (such as Expedia, MSNBC, and bCentral). In Figure 15.4, for instance, you can see that the MSNBC component includes headlines from the News, Living and Travel, Business, and three other sections.

Tip You can find out more about FrontPage at Microsoft's FrontPage Web site (http://office. microsoft.com/en-us/FX010858021033.aspx).

FIGURE 15.4   Inserting a FrontPage Web component.

FrontPage does provide some fairly advanced page components that include an ad banner manager, hit counter, search bot, hover buttons, and scheduled image and page substitutions. Most of these features, however, require FrontPage server extensions that you can download free from Microsoft's site.

> **Caution**   Be aware that if you create a Web site in FrontPage and want to publish it to the World Wide Web, you need to find a Web host that supports these server extensions. You'll learn more finding Web hosts in Lesson 16, "Making a Name for Yourself."

Macromedia Dreamweaver

Dreamweaver, too, comes packaged with an impressive array of page designs and layout templates to help you get started, although it does not feature a "looks like Microsoft Word" interface. (See Figure 15.5.) Instead, the interface includes a variety of toolbars, called *panels*, but those same panels offer a variety of ways to enhance the pages that you create.

FIGURE 15.5   A sample page in Dreamweaver.

Once you've designed a page to your specifications, you can create a template with editable and non-editable regions, which you then can use to build other pages on your site. What's more, if you change your template somewhere down the line, Dreamweaver automatically updates any page created with the template—a handy shortcut to ensure that the appearance of your site remains intact. You can use Dreamweaver's CSS Styles panel to create style sheet declarations by example and store those styles for recall in other pages. (See Figure 15.6.)

The Properties Inspector, at the bottom of the Dreamweaver workspace, enables you to review existing properties or set new properties for any page element (text, tables, images). Available properties are alignment, color, anchor tags, etc. You set the properties and Dreamweaver writes the HTML/CSS code for you.

FIGURE 15.6   The CSS Styles panel easily modifies styles. The Properties Inspector displays the properties of any selected tag.

Two of my favorite features are the Insert toolbar and Dreamweaver's new Panel groups, which appear to the right of your workspace. The panels are completely customizable, allowing you to display or hide those panels that are most frequently used by you.

- The Insert toolbar contains buttons for creating the most commonly used objects (such as images, tables, and layers).

- The CSS Styles panel contains details about the properties associated with a selected style.

- The Application panel allows you to configure databases, set up links to your remote site, and create ColdFusion components.

- The Tag Inspector panel shows you all of the attributes associated with the selected tags.

- The Files panel is similar to the Windows Explorer because it contains all of the files and folders in your Web site.

- The Frames panel visually displays the frames in your frameset helping keep you organized.

- The History panel keeps track of every action, including arrow movements, copy/paste, and text insertion that takes place on your Web page.

Dreamweaver excels at the advanced features, such as layering and XML compliance. Even though most browsers can't agree on how to support these features, Dreamweaver can check your page for compatibility with several versions of both Internet Explorer and Netscape Navigator, and verify all your internal links.

Unlike FrontPage, Dreamweaver doesn't require special server extensions or add extraneous code to your pages, which means that you are able to use your pages with any Web host.

Other Popular Web Tools

FrontPage and Dreamweaver aren't the only Web authoring and site management tools available. Several more appear in the following list:

- **Adobe GoLive** `http://www.adobe.com/products/golive/main.html`

- **NetObjects Fusion** `http://www.netobjects.com/`

- **BBEdit** `http://www.barebones.com/products/bbedit/index.shtml`

If you don't like the idea of a WYSIWYG tool and you prefer to continue working directly with the HTML source code, you probably will like HomeSite. With HomeSite, you can drag and drop HTML code, insert links, and modify existing tags. You can also search and replace HTML code, and when you're confused about which attributes apply to which tags, HomeSite can offer suggestions. All this makes HomeSite the choice of many professional developers. You can read more about HomeSite at `http://www.macromedia.com/software/homesite/`.

In this lesson, you've learned:

- Microsoft FrontPage is perfect for beginners. It looks like Microsoft Word and comes with many preformatted designs.

- Macromedia's Dreamweaver has advanced features, such as style sheet controls and layering, that make it perfect for professionals.

- Both tools enable you to create Web pages without knowing the HTML tags that you're learning in this book.

Lesson 16

Making a Name for Yourself

In this lesson, you will learn where to find a Web host to publish your Web site and tips for making sure your site is found.

Web Hosting

When you finally finish creating your Web pages, you're going to want to put them on the Internet and make sure they're found. Unless you plan to set up your own Web server, you'll probably be looking for a *Web hosting* service.

 Web Host   A company that provides space on its Web servers to store your Web files.

Web hosting services offer help in a variety of ways, and at a variety of costs. Some Web hosts offer design services, customizable scripts, visitor logs, database support, and more (in addition to the standard disk space). Use the information in Table 16.1 to find a Web host that meets your needs.

TABLE 16.1 Web Hosting Resources

Host Name	Comments	URL
The List	The official list of Internet service providers	`http://www.thelist.com/`
Web Hosting Buying Guide	CNET describes popular features offered by Web hosts so that you can decide which host is best for you	`http://reviews.cnet.com/Web_hosting_buying_guide/4520-6540_7-5138854-1.html?tag=dir`
Yahoo! Geocities	Free Web hosting with authoring resources	`http://geocities.yahoo.com/home/`
Tripod	Free Web hosting	`http://www.tripod.lycos.com/`
FreeWebs	Free Web hosting	`http://members.freewebs.com/`
Register FrontPage Hosts	Web hosts that support Microsoft FrontPage, and who have registered with Microsoft	`http://www.microsoft.com/office/frontpage/prodinfo/partner/wpp.asp`

Search Pages and Indexes

After your HTML documents are up and running on a Web server, you need to make sure that people can find them. Because most people look to *search engines* when they want to find something on the Internet, we'll start there.

 Search Engines Searchable indexes of Web resources. Some search engines (called *indexes*) also categorize information enabling people to search by categories and keywords.

Two types of search engines exist on the Web: spiders and indexes.

- A *spider* (also called a Web crawler, or *bot*, which is short for robot) is an automated script that crawls through Web pages following hyperlinks to find related pages, and then builds a database with the contents of all the pages it visits. Google.com is an example of spider technology.

- A *search directory* is a categorized list of sites on the Internet. The search directory's administrative personnel review the content of user-submitted Web sites and populate the categories. The Yahoo! directory is the best known example of this type of technology.

Search Bots

Search engine bots (also called robots, spiders, and crawlers) search through all Web pages and then index them according to the information they find. You can help the indexing portion be more accurate by using `<meta>` tags. Without `<meta>` tags, these bots treat every word in a document exactly alike. If you add keywords and descriptions to your documents, you increase the possibility that your Web pages will be found. You learned how to do this in Lesson 3, "Adding Text and More," but let's try a quick refresher. The following example shows the correct format for adding the `<meta>` tag to your documents. Figure 16.1 is an actual example of the `<meta>` tags used on the WebReference.com site.

```
<!DOCTYPE html
      PUBLIC "-//W3C//DTD XHTML 1.0 Transitional//EN"
      "http://www.w3.org/TR/xhtml1/DTD/xhtml1-
transitional.dtd">
<html xmlns="http://www.w3.org/1999/xhtml"
      xml:lang="en" lang="en">
<head>
<title>Your HTML Page</title>
<meta name="keywords" contents="keywords that
            people might use to search
            for your page.">
<meta name="description" contents="a brief
            paragraph describing your
            document.">
<meta name="author" contents="your name">
```

```
</head>
<style type="text/css">
</style>
<body>
    insert your document here.
</body>
</html>
```

FIGURE 16.1 The HTML source code for http://www.microsoft.com with the <meta> tags highlighted.

Tip If you don't add any other <meta> tags, be sure to add the description. Not all search engines rank pages in the same manner, but they all display a description of the pages found. The right description can lure visitors to your site.

Adding Your Web Site to the Search Engine

All search engines enable Web authors to add the URL of their own Web site to the search engine. Most of them do this with some type of online form. A link to Google's Advertising Programs page (http://www.google.com/submit_content.html) appears at the bottom of every Google page. (See Figure 16.2.) As you can see, Google offers several ways to advertise your Web site through its free index, or you can submit your site to specific programs for a fee. Just choose the right option for you.

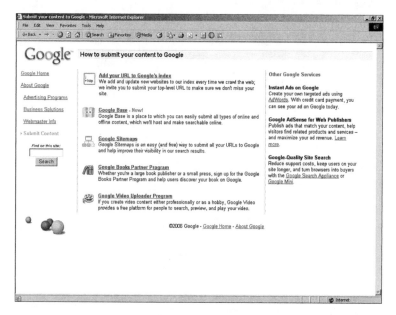

FIGURE 16.2   Google's Advertising page enables you to add your Web page to the Google index.

Yahoo!'s Suggest a Site page (http://search.yahoo.com/info/submit.html) offer similar flexibility (see Figure 16.3).

Tip Some Web sites offer to add your URL to many (if not all) search sites with one form. Companies such as Add Me (`http://www.addme.com/submission.htm`), for instance, charge a fee for this convenience. However, you probably want to add your own site information to the most popular search sites (Yahoo!, Excite, AltaVista, Lycos, LookSmart, and Go.com) to assure yourself the best chance of being found.

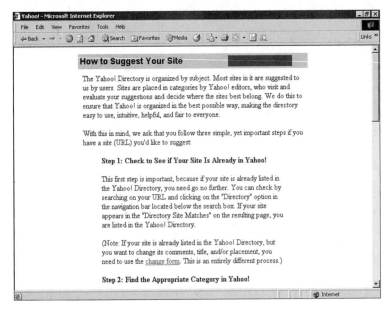

FIGURE 16.3 Yahoo!'s Suggest a Site page enables provides option for submitting your Web site.

Advertising

Don't forget that you can advertise on the Web, too. The following list of Web sites offers some form of advertising or announcement service. The flashy banner ads and annoying pop-ups page that proliferate the Web are there for a reason: People actually click on them. These advertising services can help you create your own ad and place it on pages that relate to your site. The Interactive Advertising Bureau (http://www.iab.net/standards/index.asp) maintains a set of standards for many types of Internet advertisting options.

 Tip   Remember to include your URL on your business cards, letterhead, and e-mail auto-signature. Unless you tell people where to look, they can't find you.

In this lesson, you've learned:

- Two types of search engines exist on the Web: spiders and indexes.

- To add keywords for the search engines with <meta> tags. Different search engines search for different <meta> tags, so use several (including keywords, descriptions, and author).

- Most search engines have their own site-submittal forms. Fill out these forms so that the search engine can find your site.

LESSON 17
Planning for the Future

In this lesson, you will learn what's next for the Internet and what you can do now to prepare for the coming changes.

The Future of the Internet

The extraordinary growth of the Internet since the early 1990s has come about chiefly because HTML is so easy to learn. Companies can distribute information to their employees, customers, and business partners quickly and inexpensively. Unfortunately (or fortunately, depending on your point of view), the first blush of Internet and Web development has passed and companies are already beginning to look for new ways to disseminate the information they want to share.

Hearing this cry for help, the World Wide Web Consortium has developed an eXtensible Markup Language (XML) that can be used by Web page authors whose needs extend beyond the capabilities of HTML.

 eXtensible Markup Language (XML) The newest language being developed by the World Wide Web Consortium, XML has been described as a language for defining other languages. It is more flexible than HTML.

What Is XML?

To understand XML, you need to step back and remember what HTML is. HTML is a markup language that uses a predefined set of tags to describe a document's structure in terms of paragraphs, headings, and so on. Like HTML, XML describes the structure of the document, but unlike HTML,

XML is flexible enough (or *extensible* enough) to define the same tag name (such as <title>) in several different ways depending on which *Document Type Definition (DTD)* is called.

In addition, XML takes the concept of tagging one step further by enabling developers to create custom tags and attributes. Both markup languages use style sheets to define the format of each tag with color, fonts, and emphasis.

 Document Type Definition (DTD) A file defining the set of tags that can be used within a particular file. XHTML uses three DTDs: strict, transitional, and frameset.

The following examples show how a single entry from an address book might be marked up in both HTML and XML, respectively:

- HTML:

```
<p>The White House<br />
1600 Pennsylvania Avenue NW<br />
Washington, DC  20500</p>
```

- XML:

```
<contact>
  <name>The White House</name>
  <address>1600 Pennsylvania Avenue NW</address>
   <city>Washington</city>
  <state>DC</state>
  <zip>20500</zip>
</contact>
```

Why is this difference important? It's important because, in essence, your document becomes a giant database of information.

Suppose that I am the owner of a chain of multiplex theaters and I want to put information on the Web about the movies I'm showing. In traditional Web publishing (if something as young as the World Wide Web can be said to even have a traditional method), I could do one of the following two things:

- Create a series of Web pages that would need to be updated frequently.

- Create a database that held all the information and hire a Java programmer to write an application that would enable people to perform searches on my database to see what was showing in their neighborhood.

With the advent of XML, I have a third option. I can create a single Web page that contains all the information for all my theaters, and then use style sheets and templates to present the right information to the right people.

 Tip   The W3C and industry experts are creating industry-specific versions of the XML standard. So, you can create your own tags in XML, and you can also take advantage of the fact that others in your industry are using the same standard.

Analyze the Data

The first thing I have to do is analyze my data. What information do I need to share? I probably would want to share the name of the movie, a brief description, the names of the stars in the movie, links to promotional information for the film, the name of the theater in which it's playing, the address of the theater, my phone number, the time the movie is showing, the price of the ticket, whether discounts are available, and a lot more.

After you know the type of data you need to collect, you can create your XML input document. You can see an example of two of these input documents in Figure 17.1. Each data type is represented by a pair of tags (such as <movies> and </movies>). Related data types are nested within a parent tag. For example, the <title> and <star-male> tags are related to the <movies> tag. Unlike with HTML, I made up my own XML tags based on the information I wanted to present.

FIGURE 17.1 Without a style sheet, an XML-enabled browser can only render text.

 Caution Don't rush out to convert all your HTML documents to XML just yet. Most browsers can't process XML documents yet. However, you can start preparing now by creating XHTML documents. These documents enable you to use HTML and XHMTL now, and will be easy to convert to XML in the future.

Create a Style Sheet Template

After you complete the input document, you need to create a style sheet template that determines how you present your information. You learned about style sheets in Lesson 5, "Adding Your Own Style." XML style sheet templates are very similar, but also define the structure of the document (tables, lists, paragraphs, and so on).

Tip You can learn more about XML style sheet templates from the W3C at www.w3.org/TR/xsl/. Another excellent resource for XML information is www.xml.com.

The real fun with XML documents comes from the fact that the content of the page is separated from its format. In the movie theater example, suppose that I own two movie theaters. Multiplex 1 is a downtown art theater. It only shows artsy films attended by serious film students and it likes to promote itself as a dark, almost somber, environment. Multiplex 2 is in a posh part of uptown and shows mostly revivals to an older, more conservative crowd. Now imagine that I'm planning to show the same movie, *Citizen Kane*, at both theaters.

My input document, which holds the content that appears on the Web site for both theaters, includes the following tags for *Citizen Kane*:

```
<title>Citizen Kane</title>
<star-male>Orson Wells</star-male>
<desc>Powerful newspaper owner Charles Foster Kane was many
         things to many people, both in life and, as seen in
         retrospective, in death.</desc>
<links>http://us.imdb.com/Plot?0033467</links>
```

Using XML style sheet templates, I can create two completely different pages for my theaters. For Multiplex 1, the artsy theater, I might choose to have a black background with the title in a dramatic gothic-looking font and the other elements (<star-male>, <desc>, and <links>) placed in a bulleted list below. For Multiplex 2, the revival theater, I might create a background image of a film canister for my page. Then, I might choose to place all the elements of the movie into a horizontal table for a more conservative feel.

I can do that because style sheet properties reference the element they are defining, not the content of that element. Rather than placing the content (*Citizen Kane*) on the style sheet template, I would place the following tag, which tells your computer to insert the information in the <title> tag.

```
<xsl:value-of select="title"/>
```

XML promises to be a platform-independent, software-independent language. Web developers and other programmers will be able to use the same data input documents to present information on the Web, in business automation tools (such as spreadsheets and word processors), and even on paper. That can save us all a lot of time and money.

Being Prepared

More and more, computer application developers are choosing to create their applications using Web technology. Whereas just 10 years ago, schools were busy teaching their students how to write BASIC programs and type DOS commands at the appropriate prompts, now they are teaching students HTML and learning to browse the Internet is a requirement. Some schools even offer homework help on the Internet. The Internet and Web technology are not going away, and they are going to continue to grow and change.

Already we are seeing the emergence of cell phones, pagers, and other handheld devices that can display some Internet sites. The release of the XML standard will enable the Internet to become available in any number of new media. That's why it is important to understand what you can do now to make sure that you aren't caught off guard the next time the standard changes.

Check Your Code

Microsoft and Netscape, the two largest competitors in the browser wars, continue to try and outdo each other with new browser features. Both browsers have been known to create new tags that work only on their own browser. If you use those tags when you are creating your Web site, you end up forcing your viewers to choose a browser, or lose important features that you intended to share with them. Don't put them in that position. You can use tools, such as NetMechanic (`http://www.netmechanic.com`), to ensure that your site is the best it can be.

Be sure to test your pages on different browsers and older browser versions. Not everyone uses the newest version of a browser and some older versions do not support as many tags. The Browser Photo feature at the NetMechanic site does this for a small fee. Figure 17.2 shows what you can expect from their service. For each site, Browser Photo tells you which browsers (and at what resolutions) the site was tested.

FIGURE 17.2   NetMechanic can test your pages for browser compatibility.

Use Correct Syntax

XHMTL must be well-formed; in other words, tags must be nested properly (see the "Nest Tags Properly" section later in this lesson) and tags must be closed. For example, if you forget to close your <li> (list item) tag within a <ul> (unordered or bulleted list), the browser knows that when you add the next <li> tag, you want the last one to close. In fact, you want all of your tags to close. In HTML, the following:

```
<ul>
<li>One ring-y, ding-y</li>
<li>Two ring-y, ding-ys</li>
</ul>
```

is the same as this:

```
<ul>
<li>One ring-y, ding-y
<li>Two ring-y, ding-ys
</ul>
```

and the same as this:

```
<UL>
<LI>One ring-y, ding-y</LI>
<LI>Two ring-y, ding-ys</LI>
</UL>
```

and the same as this:

```
<ul>
<Li>One ring-y, ding-y</Li>
<LI>Two ring-y, ding-ys</li>
</Ul>
```

With XHTML documents, browsers can differentiate between those examples. Only the first example is well-formed. Learn now to use the proper syntax for your documents and you won't find yourself reworking them later.

Tip Did you notice in the examples that capitalization of the tags makes a difference in XHTML? It's all part of the syntax.

Always Quote Attributes

All tag attributes must be quoted. In the past, you could add attributes, as in the following HTML sample:

```
<img src=/images/trial/gavel.jpg />
```

However, the new XHTML standard (in an effort to prepare us for the transition to XML) requires us to enclose all the attribute specifications in quotes, as in the following HTML sample:

```
<img src="/images/trial/gavel.jpg" />
```

These are minor differences, sure, but if you get into the habit of doing this correctly from the start, it will save a tremendous amount of rework as the standard is fine-tuned.

Use Style Sheets

In previous versions of HTML, Web page authors controlled the color, format, and layout of their documents with formatting tags (such as `<font color="color" size="size" family="font name">` and `<body bgcolor="color">`). With XHTML, the W3C is recommending that all these format attributes be controlled with style sheets instead.

This book has focused on the XHTML preferences, which might mean that older browsers won't always show what you intend. You can add older HTML tags to your documents without affecting your style sheets, as shown in Figure 17.3. Just remember that the HTML format tags and the style sheet properties cannot conflict, or you will have problems. If your style sheet property tells the browser that the `<body>` tag should have a yellow background, for example, be sure that the `<body>` tag also calls for a yellow background. If you choose conflicting attributes by mistake (as is done in the following example where the style sheet requires the background color to be #FFFF80, but the `<body>` tag requires the background color to be white), the style sheet property takes precedence.

Nest Tags Properly

Because XHTML and XML are more structured than HTML, you should get into the habit of paying attention to the details. You've seen in previous lessons that you can nest one HTML tag inside another. If you want to have text within a table cell (or any tagged element, such as a `<ul>`, `<li>`, and so on) to be both bold and italic, remember to close the tags in the opposite order from which they were opened. The following example shows that `<b>` was opened first and closed last.

```
<table>
<tr>
<td>
<b>This text is only bolded. <i>This text is bolded and
italicized.</i></b>
</td>
</tr>
</table>
```

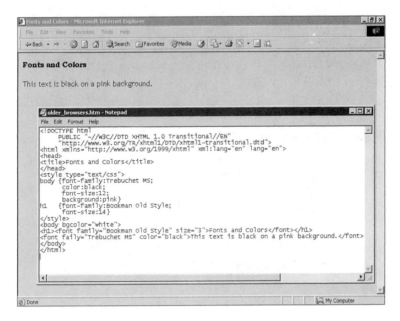

FIGURE 17.3 The HTML document seen earlier now has formatting tags added for older browsers.

As shown above, you might nest tags within a paragraph. In that code, the two sentences are both bold, although only the second is also italicized.

Check It Twice

It's such a simple thing that we often overlook it, but your pages appear more professional and your visitors have more respect for the information you provide, if your content is spelled correctly.

By the same token, don't publish broken links. Nothing is worse than clicking a link that goes nowhere, or leads to the dreaded 404 error. Make sure you verify that all your links go where you want them to go.

Caution   Whatever you do, don't forget to verify that your document includes the correct DTD: Strict, Transitional, or Frameset. The document is not XHTML-compliant if it doesn't include the DTD.

Learn All You Can

The Internet is a great place to learn about HTML, XML, and the World Wide Web. Check out some of the following great resources:

- W3C's HTML and XHTML Specifications
  www.w3.org/MarkUp/

- W3C's XML 1.0 Recommendation   www.w3.org/XML/

- XML, Java, and the Future of the Web
  http://www.ibiblio.org/pub/sun-info/standards/xml/why/xmlapps.htm

- XML Resource Center   www.xml.com

- W3 Schools   http://www.w3schools.com/default.asp

In this lesson, you've learned:

- XML goes beyond HTML. Rather than just assigning a structure to the text (with paragraphs, headings, tables, and so on), XML adds meaning and order.

- The XML standard isn't complete yet, but it will take over the Internet when it is.

- There are things you can do now to ensure that you are ready for the future of the Internet: use the correct syntax for all tags, use lowercase HTML tags, nest your tags appropriately, and use style sheets rather than the HTML formatting codes.

APPENDIX A

HTML/ XHTML Quick Reference

HTML and XHTML are markup languages that define the structure, rather than the format, of the elements of your documents. XHTML, is the latest version of that language, is more restrictive than previous versions.

Tip This appendix is based on the information provided in the *XHTML Specification W3C Recommendation* of January 26, 2000 and revised on August 1, 2002. The latest versions of these standards can be found at http://www.w3.org/TR/html/.

To make the information readily accessible, this appendix organizes HTML elements by their function in the following order:

- Required elements
- Text phrases and paragraphs
- Text formatting elements
- Lists
- Links
- Tables
- Frames

- Embedded content
- Style
- Forms
- Scripts

The elements are listed alphabetically within each section, and the following information is presented:

- **Usage**   A general description of the element.
- **Attributes**   Lists the attributes of the element with a short description of their effect.
- **Notes**   Relates any special considerations when using the element.

Caution   Several elements and attributes of HTML have been deprecated by the current XHTML specification. They have been outdated and you should avoid using them. Those deprecated elements and attributes have been eliminated in this appendix.

Following this, the common attributes and intrinsic events are summarized.

Required Elements

HTML relies on several elements to define the document as well as to provide information that is used by the browser or search engine.

Tip   Several common attributes used for structure, internationalization, and events are abbreviated as core, i18n, and events in the following quick reference sections. The description for each of these abbreviations can be found later in the "Common Attributes and Events" section.

<body>...</body>

Usage   Contains the document's content.

Attributes   `core`, `i18n`, `events`.

             `onload="..."`   Intrinsic event triggered when the doc-
             ument loads.

             `onunload="..."`   Intrinsic event triggered when the
             document unloads.

Notes   There can be only one <body>, and it must follow the
             <head>. The <body> element can be replaced by a
             <frameset> element.

<!DOCTYPE>

Usage   Version information appears on the first line of an
             HTML document and is an SGML declaration rather
             than an element.

Attributes   `html PUBLIC "-//W3C//DTD XHTML 1.0 Strict//EN"`
             `"http://www.w3.org/TR/xhtml1/DTD/xhtml1-`
             `strict.dtd">`   Used for documents following the
             Strict XHTML requirements.

             `html PUBLIC "-//W3C//DTD XHTML 1.0`
             `Transitional//EN" "http://www.w3.org/TR/`
             `xhtml1/DTD/xhtml1-transitional.dtd">`   Used for
             documents following the XHTML requirements, but
             also including some deprecated elements.

             `html PUBLIC "-//W3C//DTD XHTML 1.0`
             `Frameset//EN" "http://www.w3.org/TR/xhtml1/`
             `DTD/xhtml1-frameset.dtd">`   Used for framed
             documents.

<head>...</head>

Usage   This is the document header and contains other elements that provide information to users and search engines.

Attributes   i18n.

               profile="..."   URL specifying the location of meta data.

Notes   In general, there can be only one <head> per document. It must follow the opening <html> tag and precede the <body>. The <head> must include a <title>.

<html>...</html>

Usage   The html element contains the entire document.

Attributes   i18n.

<meta />

Usage   Provides information about the document.

Attributes   i18n.

               http-equiv="..."   HTTP response header name.

               name="..."   Name of the meta information.

               content="..."   Content of the meta information.

               -scheme="..."   Assigns a scheme to interpret the meta data.

<title>...</title>

Usage   This is the name you give your Web page. The <title> element is located in the <head> element and is displayed in the browser window title bar.

Attributes   i18n.

Text Phrases and Paragraphs

Text phrases (or blocks) can be structured to suit a specific purpose, such as creating a paragraph. This should not be confused with modifying the formatting of the text.

`<address>...</address>`

Usage
Provides a special format for author or contact information.

Attributes
`core`, `i18n`, `events`.

Notes
The `<br />` element is commonly used inside the `<address>` element to break the lines of an address.

`<blockquote>...</blockquote>`

Usage
Used to display long quotations.

Attributes
`core`, `i18n`, `events`.

`cite="..."`   The URL of the quoted text.

`<br />`

Usage
Forces a line break.

Attributes
`core`, `i18n`, `events`.

`clear="..."`   Sets the location where the next line begins after a floating object (`none`, `left`, `right`, `all`).

`<div>...</div>`

Usage
The division element is used to add structure to a block of text.

Attributes
`core`, `i18n`, `events`.

Notes
Cannot be used within a `<p>` element.

...

Usage	Emphasized text.
Attributes	`core, i18n, events.`

<h1>...</h1>–<h6>...</h6>

Usage	The six headings (`h1` is uppermost, or most important) are used in the `body` to structure information in a hierarchical fashion.
Attributes	`core, i18n, events.`
Notes	Visual browsers display the size of the headings in relation to their importance, `<h1>` being the largest and `<h6>` the smallest.

<p>...</p>

Usage	Defines a paragraph.
Attributes	`core, i18n, events.`

<pre>...</pre>

Usage	Displays preformatted text.
Attributes	`core, i18n, events.`
	`width="..."` The width of the formatted text.

...

Usage	Stronger emphasis.
Attributes	`core, i18n, events.`

`<sub>...</sub>`

Usage   Creates subscript.

Attributes   `core, i18n, events`.

`<sup>...</sup>`

Usage   Creates superscript.

Attributes   `core, i18n, events`.

Text Formatting Elements

Text characteristics such as the size, weight, and style can be modified using these elements, but the XHTML specification encourages you to use style sheets instead.

`<b>...</b>`

Usage   Bold text.

Attributes   `core, i18n, events`.

`<big>...</big>`

Usage   Large text.

Attributes   `core, i18n, events`.

`<hr />`

Usage   Horizontal rules are used to separate sections of a Web page.

Attributes   `core, events`.

`noshade="..."`   Displays the rule as a solid color.

`<i>...</i>`

Usage	Italicized text.
Attributes	`core, i18n, events.`

`<small>...</small>`

Usage	Small text.
Attributes	`core, i18n, events.`

`<tt>...</tt>`

Usage	Teletype (or monospaced) text.
Attributes	`core, i18n, events.`

Lists

You can organize text into a more structured outline by creating lists. Lists can be nested.

`<dd>...</dd>`

Usage	The definition description used in a `<dl>` (definition list) element.
Attributes	`core, i18n, events.`
Notes	Can contain block-level content, such as the `<p>` element.

`<dl>...</dl>`

Usage	Creates a definition list.
Attributes	`core, i18n, events.`
	`compact="compact"` Deprecated. Compacts the displayed list.
Notes	Must contain at least one `<dt>` or `<dd>` element in any order.

`<dt>...</dt>`

Usage	The definition term (or label) used within a `<dl>` (definition list) element.
Attributes	`core, i18n, events`.
Notes	Must contain text (which can be modified by text markup elements).

`<li>...</li>`

Usage	Defines a list item within a list.
Attributes	`core, i18n, events`.
	`type="..."` Changes the numbering style (`1, a, A, i, I`) in ordered lists, or the bullet style (`disc, square, circle`) in unordered lists.
	`value="..."` Sets the numbering to the given integer beginning with the current list item.

`<ol>...</ol>`

Usage	Creates an ordered list.
Attributes	`core, i18n, events`.
	`start="..."` Sets the starting number to the chosen integer.
Notes	Must contain at least one list item.

`<ul>...</ul>`

Usage	Creates an unordered list.
Attributes	`core, i18n, events`.
Notes	Must contain at least one list item.

Links <a>...</a>

Hyperlinking is fundamental to HTML. These elements enable you to link to other documents, other locations within a document, or external files.

Usage   Used to define links and anchors.

Attributes   core, i18n, events.

charset="..."   Character encoding of the resource.

name="..."   Defines an anchor.

href="..."   The URL of the linked resource.

target="..."   Determines where the resource is displayed (user-defined name, _blank, _parent, _self, _top).

rel="..."   Forward link types.

rev="..."   Reverse link types.

accesskey="..."   Assigns a hotkey to this element.

shape="..."   Enables you to define client-side imagemaps using defined shapes (default, rect, circle, poly).

coords="..."   Sets the size of the shape using pixel or percentage lengths.

tabindex="..."   Sets the tabbing order between elements with a defined tabindex.

Tables

Tables are meant to display data in a tabular format. Tables are also widely used for page layout purposes.

<caption>...</caption>

Usage   Displays a table caption.

Attributes   core, i18n, events.

`<table>...</table>`

Usage   Creates a table.

Attributes   `core, i18n, events.`

`width="..."`   Table width.

`cols="..."`   The number of columns.

`border="..."`   The width in pixels of a border around the table.

`frame="..."`   Sets the visible sides of a table (`void, above, below, hsides, lhs, rhs, vsides, box, border`).

`rules="..."`   Sets the visible rules within a table (`none, groups, rows, cols, all`).

`cellspacing="..."`   Spacing between cells.

`cellpadding="..."`   Spacing in cells.

`<td>...</td>`

Usage   Defines a cell's contents.

Attributes   `core, i18n, events.`

`axis="..."`   Abbreviated name.

`axes="..."`   `axis` names listing row and column headers pertaining to the cell.

`rowspan="..."`   The number of rows spanned by a cell.

`colspan="..."`   The number of columns spanned by a cell.

`char="..."`   Sets a character on which the column aligns.

`charoff="..."`   Offset to the first alignment character on a line.

<th>...</th>

Usage   Defines the cell contents of the table header.

Attributes   core, i18n, events.

axis="..."   Abbreviated name.

axes="..."   axis names listing row and column
headers pertaining to the cell.

rowspan="..."   The number of rows spanned by a
cell.

colspan="..."   The number of columns spanned by a
cell.

char="..."   Sets a character on which the column
aligns.

charoff="..."   Offset to the first alignment character
on a line.

<tr>...</tr>

Usage   Defines a row of table cells.

Attributes   core, i18n, events.

char="..."   Sets a character on which the column
aligns.

charoff="..."   Offset to the first alignment character
on a line.

Frames

Frames create new panels in the Web browser window that are used to
display content from different source documents.

`<frame />`

Usage   Defines a frame.

Attributes `name="..."`   The name of a frame.

`src="..."`   The source to be displayed in a frame.

`frameborder="..."`   Toggles the border between frames (`0`, `1`).

`marginwidth="..."`   Sets the space between the frame border and content.

`marginheight="..."`   Sets the space between the frame border and content.

`noresize`   Disables sizing.

`scrolling="..."`   Determines scrollbar presence (`auto`, `yes`, `no`).

Notes   Use the Frameset DTD.

`<frameset>...</frameset>`

Usage   Defines the layout of frames within a window.

Attributes `rows="..."`   The number of rows.

`cols="..."`   The number of columns.

`onload="..."`   The intrinsic event triggered when the document loads.

`onunload="..."`   The intrinsic event triggered when the document unloads.

Notes   Use the Frameset DTD.

`<iframe>...</iframe>`

Usage   Creates an inline frame.

Attributes `name="..."`   The name of the frame.

src="..."   The source to be displayed in a frame.

frameborder="..."   Toggles the border between frames (0, 1).

marginwidth="..."   Sets the space between the frame border and content.

marginheight="..."   Sets the space between the frame border and content.

scrolling="..."   Determines scrollbar presence (auto, yes, no).

height="..."   Height.

width="..."   Width.

<noframes>...</noframes>

Usage   Alternative content when frames are not supported.

Attributes   None.

Notes   Use the Frameset DTD. The <body> element must be included inside the <noframes> tag.

Embedded Content

Also called inclusions, embedded content applies to Java applets, imagemaps, and other multimedia or programmed content that is placed in a Web page to provide additional functionality.

Comments <!-- ... -->

Usage   Used to insert notes or scripts that are not displayed by the browser.

Attributes   None.

Notes   Comments are not restricted to one line and can be any length. The end tag is not required to be on the same line as the start tag.

`<img />`

Usage   Includes an image in the document.

Attributes   `core`, `i18n`, `events`.

            `src="..."`   The URL of the image.

            `alt="..."`   Alternative text to display.

            `height="..."`   The height of the image.

            `width="..."`   The width of the image.

            `border="..."`   Border width.

            `hspace="..."`   The horizontal space separating the image from other content.

            `vspace="..."`   The vertical space separating the image from other content.

            `usemap="..."`   The URL to a client-side imagemap.

            `ismap="ismap"`   Identifies a server-side imagemap.

`<map>...</map>`

Usage   When used with the `<area>` element, it creates a client-side imagemap.

Attributes   `core`.

            `name="..."`   The name of the imagemap to be created.

`<object>...</object>`

Usage   Includes an object or applet.

Attributes   `core`, `i18n`, `events`.

            `declare="declare"`   A flag that declares, but doesn't create an object.

classid="..."   The URL of the object's location.

codebase="..."   The URL for resolving URLs specified by other attributes.

data="..."   The URL to the object's data.

type="..."   The Internet content type for data.

codetype="..."   The Internet content type for the code.

standby="..."   Shows message while loading.

height="..."   The height of the object.

width="..."   The width of the object.

border="..."   Displays the border around an object.

hspace="..."   The space between the sides of the object and other page content.

vspace="..."   The space between the top and bottom of the object and other page content.

usemap="..."   The URL to an imagemap.

shapes=   Enables you to define areas to search for hyperlinks if the object is an image.

name="..."   The URL to submit as part of a form.

tabindex="..."   Sets the tabbing order between elements with a defined tabindex.

Style <style>...</style>

Style sheets (both embedded and linked) are incorporated into an HTML document through the use of the <style> element.

Usage   Creates an internal style sheet.

Attributes   i18n.

type="..."   The Internet content type.

media="..."   Defines the destination medium
(screen, print, projection, braille, speech, all).

title="..."   The title of the style.

Notes   Located within the <head> element.

Forms

Forms create an interface for the user to select options and return data to
the Web server.

<button>...</button>

Usage   Creates a button.

Attributes   core, i18n, events.

name="..."   The button name.

value="..."   The value of the button.

type="..."   The button type (button, submit, reset).

disabled="..."   Sets the button state to disabled.

tabindex="..."   Sets the tabbing order between
elements with a defined tabindex.

onfocus="..."   The event that occurs when the
element receives focus.

onblur="..."   The event that occurs when the
element loses focus.

<form>...</form>

Usage   Creates a form that holds controls for user input.

Attributes   core, i18n, events.

action="..."   The URL for the server action.

`method="..."`   The HTTP method (get, post). get is deprecated.

`enctype="..."`   Specifies the MIME (Internet media type).

`onsubmit="..."`   The intrinsic event that occurs when the form is submitted.

`onreset="..."`   The intrinsic event that occurs when the form is reset.

`target="..."`   Determines where the resource is displayed (user-defined name, _blank, _parent, _self, _top).

`accept-charset="..."`   The list of character encodings.

`<input />`

Usage   Defines controls used in forms.

Attributes   `core, i18n, events.`

`type="..."`   The type of input control (text, password, checkbox, radio, submit, reset, file, hidden, image, button).

`name="..."`   The name of the control (required except for submit and reset).

`value="..."`   The initial value of the control (required for radio and checkboxes).

`checked="checked"`   Sets the radio buttons to a checked state.

`disabled="..."`   Disables the control.

`readonly="..."`   For text password types.

`size="..."`   The width of the control in pixels except for text and password controls, which are specified in number of characters.

`maxlength="..."` The maximum number of characters that can be entered.

`src="..."` The URL to an image control type.

`alt="..."` An alternative text description.

`usemap="..."` The URL to a client-side imagemap.

`tabindex="..."` Sets the tabbing order between elements with a defined `tabindex`.

`onfocus="..."` The event that occurs when the element receives focus.

`onblur="..."` The event that occurs when the element loses focus.

`onselect="..."` Intrinsic event that occurs when the control is selected.

`onchange="..."` Intrinsic event that occurs when the control is changed.

`accept="..."` File types allowed for upload.

`<label>...</label>`

Usage   Labels a control.

Attributes   `core, i18n, events.`

`for="..."` Associates a label with an identified control.

`disabled="..."` Disables a control.

`accesskey="..."` Assigns a hotkey to this element.

`onfocus="..."` The event that occurs when the element receives focus.

`onblur="..."` The event that occurs when the element loses focus.

`<legend>...</legend>`

Usage   Assigns a caption to a `fieldset`.

Attributes   `core, i18n, events`.

`accesskey="..."`   Assigns a hotkey to this element.

`<option>...</option>`

Usage   Specifies choices in a `<select>` element.

Attributes   `core, i18n, events`.

`selected="selected"`   Specifies whether the option is selected.

`disabled="disabled"`   Disables the control.

`value="..."`   The value submitted if a control is submitted.

`<select>...</select>`

Usage   Creates choices for the user to select.

Attributes   `core, i18n, events`.

`name="..."`   The name of the element.

`size="..."`   The height in number of visible rows.

`multiple="multiple"`   Allows multiple selections.

`disabled="disabled"`   Disables the control.

`tabindex="..."`   Sets the tabbing order between elements with a defined `tabindex`.

`onfocus="..."`   The event that occurs when the element receives focus.

`onblur="..."`   The event that occurs when the element loses focus.

`onselect="..."`   Intrinsic event that occurs when the control is selected.

`onchange="..."`   Intrinsic event that occurs when the control is changed.

`<textarea>...</textarea>`

Usage   Creates an area for user input with multiple lines.

Attributes   `core, i18n, events`.

`name="..."`   The name of the control.

`rows="..."`   The height in number of rows.

`cols="..."`   The width in number of columns.

`disabled="disabled"`   Disables the control.

`readonly="readonly"`   Sets the displayed text to read-only status.

`tabindex="..."`   Sets the tabbing order between elements with a defined `tabindex`.

`onfocus="..."`   The event that occurs when the element receives focus.

`onblur="..."`   The event that occurs when the element loses focus.

`onselect="..."`   Intrinsic event that occurs when the control is selected.

`onchange="..."`   Intrinsic event that occurs when the control is changed.

Notes   Text to be displayed is placed within the start and end tags.

Scripts

Scripting language is made available to process data and performs other dynamic events through the <script> element.

<script>...</script>

Usage   The <script> element contains client-side scripts that are executed by the browser.

Attributes   type="..."   Script language Internet content type.

             src="..."   The URL for the external script.

Notes   You can set the default scripting language in the <meta /> element.

<noscript>...</noscript>

Usage   Provides alternative content for browsers unable to execute a script.

Attributes   None.

Common Attributes and Events

Four attributes are abbreviated as core. They are

- id="..."   A global identifier.

- class="..."   A list of classes separated by spaces.

- style="..."   Style information.

- title="..."   Provides more information for a specific element, as opposed to the <title> element, which entitles the entire Web page.

Two attributes for internationalization (i18n) are abbreviated as i18n:

- lang="..."   The language identifier.

- dir=c   The text direction (ltr, rtl).

The following intrinsic events are abbreviated events:

- OnClick="..."   A pointing device (such as a mouse) was single-clicked.

- OnDblClick="..."   A pointing device (such as a mouse) was double-clicked.

- OnMouseDown="..."   A mouse button was clicked and held down.

- OnMouseUp="..."   A mouse button that was clicked and held down was released.

- OnMouseOver="..."   A mouse moved the cursor over an object.

- OnMouseMove="..."   The mouse was moved.

- OnMouseOut="..."   A mouse moved the cursor off an object.

- OnKeyPress="..."   A key was pressed and released.

- OnKeyDown="..."   A key was pressed and held down.

- OnKeyUp="..."   A key that was pressed has been released.

APPENDIX B

Style Sheet Quick Reference

Cascading Style Sheets enable Web authors to attach styles (for example, fonts, spacing, and colors) to HTML documents. By separating the presentation style of documents from the content of documents, the style sheet specification simplifies Web authoring and site maintenance. This appendix provides a quick reference to some of the most common style sheet properties.

Note This appendix is based on the information provided in the *CSS 2.1 Specification W3C Recommendation* (revised on June 15, 2005). The latest version of this standard can be found at www.w3.org/TR/CSS21/.

To make the information readily accessible, this appendix organizes style sheet properties by their function in the following order:

- Text and fonts
- Typography
- Colors and backgrounds
- Borders and tables
- Lists
- Layout

The elements are listed alphabetically within each section, and the following information is presented:

- **Usage**   A general description of the property.

- **Values**   Lists the values of the property with a short description of their effect.

- **Initial Value**   Lists the default value of the property. It is not necessary to set this value.

- **Notes**   Relates any special considerations when using the property.

Text and Fonts

Sets the fonts, colors, positioning, and other styles for the text elements.

> **Tip**   Links can use all the same properties as other text elements, but you need to remember the link types:
>
> - a:link
> - a:visited
> - a:active
> - a:hover

font-family

Usage   Sets the font to be used.

Values   <family name>   The name of the font family (such as Arial) as it appears in your editor.

<generic family>   Sets a generic font set dependent on the user's computer (such as, serif, sans-serif, cursive, fantasy, and monospace).

inherit   The same as the parent element.

Initial Value Depends on the browser setting.

Tip   Because not all computer systems ship with the same fonts, there are only a few sure-fire fonts worth specifying:

- Arial
- Arial Black
- Comic Sans
- Courier New
- Georgia

- Impact
- Times New Roman
- Trebuchet
- Verdana

font-size

Usage   Sets the font size.

Values   *<absolute-size>*   The size of the font expressed in points (pt), inches (in), centimeters (cm), pixels (px), or one of the absolute keywords (xx-small, x-small, small, medium, large, x-large, xx-large, smaller, or larger) which determines the size of the font relative to the default value.

              inherit   The same as the parent element.

Initial Value   medium; typically 12 points.

font-style

Usage   Sets the style of the font.

Values   normal   No special format to the font.

              italic   The font appears in italics.

              inherit   The same as the parent element.

Initial Value   normal.

font-weight

Usage   Sets the weight of the font.

Values   `<weight>`   The weight of the font may be `extra-light`, `light`, `demi-light`, `medium`, `normal`, `demi-bold`, `bold`, or `extra-bold`.

`<relative-weight>`   The weight of the font may be relative to some inherited value (for example, `bolder` or `lighter`)

`100–900`   The weight of the font as a specific numerical value, where `400` is approximately the same as normal and `700` is approximately the same as bold.

`inherit`   The same as the parent element.

Initial Value   `normal`.

font-variant

Usage   Changes the appearance of the font.

Values   `small-caps`   Transforms all text into small caps.

`inherit`   The same as the parent element.

Initial Value   `normal`.

text-decoration

Usage   Sets the format of the text element.

Values   `underline`   A line appears under the text.

`overline`   A line appears over the text.

`line-through`   A line appears horizontally through the center of the text.

`blink`   The text blinks.

`inherit`   The same as the parent element.

Initial Value   `none` (or `underline` for links).

text-transform

Usage	Sets the format of the text element.
Values	`capitalize` Transforms the case of the first letter of every word to uppercase.
	`uppercase` All text appears uppercase.
	`lowercase` All text appears lowercase.
	`inherit` The same as the parent element.
Initial Value	`none`.

Typography

This sets the style that determines the spacing and alignment of text elements.

word-spacing

Usage	Sets the spacing between words.
Values	`<length>` The spacing may be expressed in inches (`in`), centimeters (`cm`), points (`pt`), and pixels (`px`).
	`inherit` The same as the parent element.
Initial Value	`normal`

letter-spacing

Usage	Sets the spacing between letters, also known as kerning.
Values	`<length>` The spacing may be expressed in inches (`in`), centimeters (`cm`), points (`pt`), and pixels (`px`).
	`inherit` The same as the parent element.
Initial Value	`normal`

line-height

Usage   Sets the total height of a line of text, including the space above and below the text.

Values   `<length>` The spacing may be expressed in inches (`in`), centimeters (`cm`), points (`pt`), and pixels (`px`).

                   `inherit` The same as the parent element.

Initial Value   `normal`

 Tip   Each of these properties may also be expressed as a negative (for example, `letter-spacing:-10px`), which decreases the normal spacing to create interesting effects.

text-align

Usage   Sets the alignment of the text element.

Values   `left` The text is aligned on the left side.

                   `right` The text is aligned on the right side.

                   `center` The text is centered.

                   `justify` The text is aligned on both the left and right sides.

                   `inherit` The same as the parent element.

Initial Value   Depends on the browser settings.

vertical-align

Usage   Sets the vertical alignment of the element relative to the surrounding elements.

Values   `baseline` The element aligns with the baseline of surrounding elements.

                   `sub` or `super` The element is subscripted or superscripted respectively.

top, middle, bottom   The element is aligned with the top, middle, or bottom of surrounding elements respectively.

text-top or text-bottom   The element is aligned with the top or bottom of surrounding text elements.

inherit   The same as the parent element.

Initial Value   baseline.

text-indent

Usage   Sets the spacing before the text element relative to the surrounding elements.

Values   <length>   The indent spacing is a fixed length expressed in inches (in), centimeters (cm), points (pt), or pixels (px).

<percentage>   The indent spacing is a percentage of the containing element (usually the browser window or the table cell).

inherit   The same as the parent element.

Initial Value   0.

Colors and Backgrounds

This sets the style for the background of the text, page, table, or other elements.

Caution   As with other elements, color does not appear the same on all computers; however, most monitors will display a 256-color palette (with 216 of those colors consistent across all platforms). Lynda Weinmann's website (www.lynda.com/hex.html) contains two charts sorting these browser-safe colors sorted by both value and hue. They are well worth checking out.

background-color

Usage   Sets the background color of an element.

Values   `<color>` The hex number (or text equivalent) of the preferred color.

               `transparent` The same background as the underlying element.

Initial Value `transparent`

background-image

Usage   Sets the background image for an element.

Values   `url("...")` The URL for the background image.

               `none` No image.

Initial Value `none`

background-position

Usage   Sets the position of the background image. The values always appear in pairs—the first number refers to the horizontal positioning of the image; the second to the vertical positioning. For example, `background-position: 0% 100%` will place the image at the top right of the browser window.

Values   `<percentage>` The position of the background image.

               `top` Corresponds to 0%.

               `bottom` Corresponds to 100%.

               `left` Corresponds to 0%.

               `right` Corresponds to 100%.

               `center` Corresponds to 50%.

Initial Value `none`.

background-repeat

Usage   Sets the pattern of repeats for the background image.

Values   `<no-repeat>`   The background image does not repeat.

                `<repeat>`   The background image repeats both horizontally and vertically (as normal) to fill the entire space.

                `<repeat-x>`   The background image repeats horizontally only to fill the entire space.

                `<repeat-y>`   The background image repeats vertically only to fill the entire space.

Initial Value   `repeat`.

color

Usage   Sets the color of the font.

Values   `<color>`   The hex number (or text equivalent) of the preferred color.

                `inherit`   The same as the parent element.

Initial Value   Depends on the browser setting.

Tip   Some colors have been defined in the style sheet specification by a name, not a hexadecimal code. The following 16 are guaranteed to appear the same in all resolutions.

• aqua	• gray	• navy	• silver
• black	• green	• olive	• teal
• blue	• lime	• purple	• white
• fuchsia	• maroon	• red	• yellow

Borders and Tables

These set the border styles for the page, text, table, and image elements.

border-color

Usage	Sets the border color for an element.
Values	`<color>` The hex number (or text equivalent) of the preferred color.
	`inherit` The same as the parent element.
	`none` No image.
Initial Value	`transparent`.
Notes	Set the color for specific borders using the `border-top-color`, `border-right-color`, `border-bottom-color`, and `border-left-color` properties.

border-style

Usage	Sets the style of the border for an element.
Values	`dotted` A series of small dots form the border.
	`dashed` A series of dashes form the border.
	`solid` A narrow, solid line forms the border.
	`double` Double, narrow, solid lines form the border.
	`groove` A narrow carved line forms the border.
	`ridge` A narrow raised line forms the border.
	`inset` The border makes the entire element appear to be embedded.
	`outset` The border makes the entire element appear to be raised.
	`inherit` The same as the parent element.
	`none` No border.
Initial Value	`none`.
Notes	Set the position of the border with the `border-top-style`, `border-right-style`, `border-bottom-style`, and `border-left-style` properties.

border-width

Usage	Sets the width of the border for an element.
Values	<width> The width is a fixed length expressed in inches (in), centimeters (cm), points (pt), or pixels (px).
	thin A thin line forms the border.
	medium A medium line forms the border.
	thick A thick line forms the border.
	inherit The same as the parent element.
Initial Value	medium.
Notes	Set the width of specific borders using the border-top-width, border-right-width, border-bottom-width, and border-left-width properties.

caption-side

Usage	Sets the position of the caption relative to the table.
Values	top The caption appears at the top of the table.
	bottom The caption appears at the bottom of the table.
	inherit The same as the parent element.
Initial Value	0.

empty-cells

Usage	Specifies the treatment of empty table cells.
Values	show Empty cells are treated the same as nonempty cells.
	hide Empty cells are not displayed.
	inherit The same as the parent element.
Initial Value	show.

float

Usage   Sets the spacing before the text element relative to the surrounding elements.

Values   `left`   The content of the element floats to the left.

`right`   The content of the element floats to the right.

`none`   The content does not float.

`inherit`   The same as the parent element.

Initial Value   `none`.

Lists

These styles set styles (for example, the bullet type) for ordered and unordered lists. Combine these styles with margins and indents.

list-style-image

Usage   Sets an image to replace the list bullets.

Values   `url("...")`   The URL for the image.

`none`   No images.

`inherit`   The same as the parent element.

Initial Value   `none`

list-style-type

Usage   Sets the style of the unordered list bullets (or numbers in ordered lists).

Values   `<shape>`   The bullets can be set to `disc` (closed circle), `circle` (open circle), or `square` (closed square).

`<alignment>`   The bullets can be aligned around `decimal` or `decimal-leading-zero`.

<text>   Numbers in an ordered list can be Roman numerals (lower-roman, upper-roman), Latin numerals (lower-latin, upper-latin), or American alphabet characters (lower-alpha, upper-alpha).

inherit   The same as the parent element.

Initial Value   disc.

Layout

These styles can be used in combination with any of the previous style types to affect the entire page, or components of the page.

margin

Usage   Sets the margins for the page.

Values   <margin-width>   The width of the margin in percentage or in fixed width.

inherit   The same as the parent element.

Initial Value   0.

Notes   Set specific margins using the margin-top, margin-right, margin-bottom, and margin-left properties.

padding

Usage   Sets the space that surrounds the element.

Values   <length>   Sets the table padding to a fixed length.

<percentage>   Sets the table padding to a percentage.

Initial Value   0.

Notes   Set specific padding using the padding-top, padding-right, padding-bottom, and padding-left properties.

APPENDIX C

Special Characters

Symbols (such as & and ') are used in everyday writing. HTML uses a shorthand code to display certain characters correctly. The most frequently used characters are referenced in the following tables. As with any code, review your finished pages in the browser before sending your work to the Internet.

 Caution The entity references in the tables that follow are case sensitive.

Symbol Entities

Character	Description	Entity Reference	Entity Number
"	quotation mark	&quot;	&#34;
'	apostrophe	' (does not work in IE)	&#39;
&	ampersand	&amp;	&#38;
<	less-than	&lt;	&#60;
>	greater-than	&gt;	&#62;
	non-breaking space		
¡	inverted exclamation mark	&iexcl;	&#161;

continues

Character	Description	Entity Reference	Entity Number
☐	currency	&curren;	&#164;
¢	cent	&cent;	&#162;
£	pound	&pound;	&#163;
¥	yen	&yen;	&#165;
¦	broken vertical bar	&brvbar;	&#166;
§	section	&sect;	&#167;
¨	spacing diaeresis	&uml;	&#168;
©	copyright	&copy;	&#169;
ª	feminine ordinal indicator	&ordf;	&#170;
«	angle quotation mark (left)	&laquo;	&#171;
¬	negation	&not;	&#172;
	soft hyphen	&shy;	&#173;
®	registered trademark	&reg;	&#174;
™	trademark	&trade;	&#8482;
¯	spacing macron	&macr;	&#175;
°	degree	&deg;	&#176;
±	plus-or-minus	&plusmn;	&#177;
²	superscript 2	&sup2;	&#178;
³	superscript 3	&sup3;	&#179;
´	spacing acute	&acute;	&#180;
µ	micro	&micro;	&#181;
¶	paragraph	&para;	&#182;
·	middle dot	&middot;	&#183;
¸	spacing cedilla	&cedil;	&#184;

Character	Description	Entity Reference	Entity Number
¹	superscript 1	¹	¹
º	masculine ordinal indicator	º	º
»	angle quotation mark (right)	»	»
¼	fraction 1/4	¼	¼
½	fraction 1/2	½	½
¾	fraction 3/4	¾	¾
¿	inverted question mark	¿	¿
×	multiplication	×	×
÷	division	÷	÷

Character Entities

Character	Description	Entity Reference	Entity Number
À	capital a, grave accent	À	À
Á	capital a, acute accent	Á	Á
Â	capital a, circumflex accent	Â	Â
Ã	capital a, tilde	Ã	Ã
Ä	capital a, umlaut mark	Ä	Ä
Å	capital a, ring	Å	Å
Æ	capital ae	Æ	Æ
Ç	capital c, cedilla	Ç	Ç
È	capital e, grave accent	È	È
É	capital e, acute accent	É	É

continues

Character	Description	Entity Reference	Entity Number
Ê	capital e, circumflex accent	Ê	Ê
Ë	capital e, umlaut mark	Ë	Ë
Ì	capital i, grave accent	Ì	Ì
Í	capital i, acute accent	Í	Í
Î	capital i, circumflex accent	Î	Î
Ï	capital i, umlaut mark	Ï	Ï
Ð	capital eth, Icelandic	Ð	Ð
Ñ	capital n, tilde	Ñ	Ñ
Ò	capital o, grave accent	Ò	Ò
Ó	capital o, acute accent	Ó	Ó
Ô	capital o, circumflex accent	Ô	Ô
Õ	capital o, tilde	Õ	Õ
Ö	capital o, umlaut mark	Ö	Ö
Ø	capital o, slash	Ø	Ø
Ù	capital u, grave accent	Ù	Ù
Ú	capital u, acute accent	Ú	Ú
Û	capital u, circumflex accent	Û	Û
Ü	capital u, umlaut mark	Ü	Ü
Ý	capital y, acute accent	Ý	Ý
Þ	capital THORN, Icelandic	Þ	Þ
ß	small sharp s, German	ß	ß
à	small a, grave accent	à	à
á	small a, acute accent	á	á
â	small a, circumflex accent	â	â
ã	small a, tilde	ã	ã
ä	small a, umlaut mark	ä	ä

Character	Description	Entity Reference	Entity Number
å	small a, ring	&aring;	&#229;
æ	small ae	&aelig;	&#230;
ç	small c, cedilla	&ccedil;	&#231;
è	small e, grave accent	&egrave;	&#232;
é	small e, acute accent	&eacute;	&#233;
ê	small e, circumflex accent	&ecirc;	&#234;
ë	small e, umlaut mark	&euml;	&#235;
ì	small i, grave accent	&igrave;	&#236;
í	small i, acute accent	&iacute;	&#237;
î	small i, circumflex accent	&icirc;	&#238;
ï	small i, umlaut mark	&iuml;	&#239;
ð	small eth, Icelandic	&eth;	&#240;
ñ	small n, tilde	&ntilde;	&#241;
ò	small o, grave accent	&ograve;	&#242;
ó	small o, acute accent	&oacute;	&#243;
ô	small o, circumflex accent	&ocirc;	&#244;
õ	small o, tilde	&otilde;	&#245;
ö	small o, umlaut mark	&ouml;	&#246;
ø	small o, slash	&oslash;	&#248;
ù	small u, grave accent	&ugrave;	&#249;
ú	small u, acute accent	&uacute;	&#250;
û	small u, circumflex accent	&ucirc;	&#251;
ü	small u, umlaut mark	&uuml;	&#252;
ý	small y, acute accent	&yacute;	&#253;
þ	small thorn, Icelandic	&thorn;	&#254;
ÿ	small y, umlaut mark	&yuml;	&#255;

Greek Entities

Character	Description	Entity Reference	Entity Number
A	Greek capital letter alpha	&Alpha;	&#913;
B	Greek capital letter beta	&Beta;	&#914;
Γ	Greek capital letter gamma	&Gamma;	&#915;
Δ	Greek capital letter delta	&Delta;	&#916;
E	Greek capital letter epsilon	&Epsilon;	&#917;
Z	Greek capital letter zeta	&Zeta;	&#918;
H	Greek capital letter eta	&Eta;	&#919;
Θ	Greek capital letter theta	&Theta;	&#920;
I	Greek capital letter iota	&Iota;	&#921;
K	Greek capital letter kappa	&Kappa;	&#922;
Λ	Greek capital letter lambda	&Lambda;	&#923;
M	Greek capital letter mu	&Mu;	&#924;
N	Greek capital letter nu	&Nu;	&#925;
Ξ	Greek capital letter xi	&Xi;	&#926;
O	Greek capital letter omicron	&Omicron;	&#927;
Π	Greek capital letter pi	&Pi;	&#928;
P	Greek capital letter rho	&Rho;	&#929;
Σ	Greek capital letter sigma	&Sigma;	&#931;
T	Greek capital letter tau	&Tau;	&#932;
Υ	Greek capital letter upsilon	&Upsilon;	&#933;
Φ	Greek capital letter phi	&Phi;	&#934;
X	Greek capital letter chi	&Chi;	&#935;
Ψ	Greek capital letter psi	&Psi;	&#936;

Character	Description	Entity Reference	Entity Number
Ω	Greek capital letter omega	Ω	Ω
α	Greek small letter alpha	α	α
β	Greek small letter beta	β	β
γ	Greek small letter gamma	γ	γ
δ	Greek small letter delta	δ	δ
ε	Greek small letter epsilon	ε	ε
ζ	Greek small letter zeta	ζ	ζ
η	Greek small letter eta	η	η
θ	Greek small letter theta	θ	θ
ι	Greek small letter iota	ι	ι
κ	Greek small letter kappa	κ	κ
λ	Greek small letter lambda	λ	λ
μ	Greek small letter mu	μ	μ
ν	Greek small letter nu	ν	ν
ξ	Greek small letter xi	ξ	ξ
o	Greek small letter omicron	ο	ο
π	Greek small letter pi	π	π
ρ	Greek small letter rho	ρ	ρ
ς	Greek small letter final sigma	ς	ς
σ	Greek small letter sigma	σ	σ
τ	Greek small letter tau	τ	τ
υ	Greek small letter upsilon	υ	υ
φ	Greek small letter phi	φ	φ
χ	Greek small letter chi	χ	χ

continues

Character	Description	Entity Reference	Entity Number
ψ	Greek small letter psi	&psi;	&#968;
ω	Greek small letter omega	&omega;	&#969;
φ	Greek small letter theta symbol	ϑ (does not work in IE)	&#977;
γ	Greek upsilon with hook symbol	ϒ (does not work in IE)	&#978;
ϖ	Greek pi symbol	ϖ (does not work in IE)	&#982;

Other Entities

Character	Description	Entity Reference	Entity Number
Œ	capital ligature OE	&OElig;	&#338;
œ	small ligature oe	&oelig;	&#339;
Š	capital S with caron	&Scaron;	&#352;
š	small S with caron	&scaron;	&#353;
Ÿ	capital Y with diaeres	&Yuml;	&#376;
ˆ	modifier letter circumflex accent	&circ;	&#710;
˜	small tilde	&tilde;	&#732;
	en space		
	em space		
	thin space		

Character	Description	Entity Reference	Entity Number
–	en dash	–	–
—	em dash	—	—
'	left single quotation mark	‘	‘
'	right single quotation mark	’	’
‚	single low-9 quotation mark	‚	‚
"	left double quotation mark	“	“
"	right double quotation mark	”	”
„	double low-9 quotation mark	„	„
†	dagger	†	†
‡	double dagger	‡	‡
…	horizontal ellipsis	…	…
‰	per mille	‰	‰
‹	single left-pointing angle quotation	‹	‹
›	single right-pointing angle quotation	›	›
∈	euro	€	€

INDEX

SYMBOLS

A

B

D

X–Z